Dialogues on Women

Dialogues on Women

Images of Women in the History of Philosophy

L.D. Derksen

VU University Press
Amsterdam 1996

VU University Press is an imprint of:
VU Boekhandel/Uitgeverij bv
De Boelelaan 1105
1081 HV Amsterdam
The Netherlands

tel. (020) - 644 43 55
fax (020) - 646 27 19

isbn 90-5383-460-5

Table of Contents

Preface

The main source of inspiration for writing this book is the Research Group Women's Studies, Department of Philosophy, Vrije Universiteit Amsterdam of which I have been a member since its founding in 1983. I selected the philosophical literature discussed in this book from among the texts which we read over the years and many theoretical issues raised here emerged out of the discussions we held. Later, the members of the group were so kind as to discuss and comment on the entire manuscript. Some people had already experienced the earlier rounds of discussions and I would like to thank them for their patience and valuable suggestions. My thanks goes out to Trix Bakker, Ymkje de Boer, Erica Drewes-Wentink, Tine Greidanus, Frederike de Jong, Anna Kant-Koolma, Marya Mourits-de Haas, Mariëtte Willemsen, and Diet Zijlstra-Grosheide. I would like to mention especially our chairperson, Atie Brüggemann-Kruijff for her valuable contributions.

I would also like to thank the former head of the philosophy library of the Vrije Universiteit, the late Marius Bremmer, for his support in ordering literature pertaining to this research. I had told him that I would mention his name in this book and he was, as always, enthusiastic.

Above all, I would like to thank my parents for their loving support.

Introduction

The point of departure for writing this book is the premise that philosophers in the past have written on the question of the nature of women and their role in society and that what they wrote was read by other philosophers who in turn reacted to the views presented. I am prepared to admit that the philosophical dialogue on women was never an extensive part of philosophical systems but, almost without exception, philosophers did speak about women. As such, this fact need not be at all surprising. For many philosophers, a view of women was part and parcel of a view on human nature and society. If we ask the question "What is man?" we must consider the nature and significance of the male-female distinction. If we want to consider the nature of the social, political and ethical, we need to concern ourselves with questions surrounding the spheres of the public and private, the home, family and state, the roles which people are to have in society. Even questions which do not at first glance seem to concern the male-female distinction, such as: what is the nature and scope of reason and emotions? the ultimate nature of reality itself? are connected to male and female by some philosophers. The masculine and the feminine have been used as allegorical or symbolical representations of human capacities and aspects of reality.

In this book, a number of ways in which philosophers speak of women are discussed. There is a historical line and at the same time every chapter has its own theme through which another aspect of speaking about the feminine emerges.

In the first chapter, I argue that the patriarchal system is basic to western society. Because this system has so much influence on the perception of the nature and social roles of women, discussions concerning women are usually held in response to the power of patriarchy. First, I show that there are patriarchal theories which go back to the very beginning of western philosophy, that is, to the Pythagorean school. In this school, women wrote on their roles as mothers and housewives in light of Pythagorean philosophical principles. The emphasis in this chapter is on the ethical demands which the traditional patriarchal family structure makes on women, or, more traditionally speaking, on the "virtues" demanded of women functioning in this structure. In the second part of this chapter, I discuss philosophical theories on the origin and power of patriarchy.

In the second and third chapters, on Plato and Aristotle, I show that questions concerning the nature of women were answered by means of theories on the nature of the human soul. The answers were used to determine the capacity of individuals to play their roles in society. Plato and Aristotle differ in their views of the nature of women and we shall see the implications of this for their theories of society.

For the philosophers of the patristic and medieval period, the nature of women was analysed in terms of the philosophical and theological implications of the Bible stories and thus the discourse on women enters into the realm of the theological. Philosophers of this period discussed the implications for a view on women the story of Adam and Eve, the fall into sin, the resulting curses on mankind, the role of Mary in the history of salvation, the female virtues, the nature of marriage, and the contributions which women could make to religious life. A contrast will be sketched between the views of St. Thomas Aquinas, discussed in chapter four, and those of Christine de Pizan, whose views are presented in chapter five.

In the early modern period, with the rise of modern science and the emphasis on reason as opposed to tradition, the issue was raised as to the equal access to knowledge for women. In chapter six, the relationship between the development of "the new science" and views of women is discussed with reference to Bacon and Descartes. The conclusions these two thinkers draw are very different: Bacon sees reason and science as masculine, and nature as feminine, while Descartes supports the notion of *sensus communis*, the universal capacity of all people to know the truth of reality and to think rationally. In this period, in contrast to the Middle Ages, there is perhaps a hardening of attitudes towards admitting women to academic pursuits. At the same time, however, the first steps were taken by women to use their reason and its results in the public realm, such as having an academic education or literary employment.

In the seventh chapter, I show how in the 18th century, Rousseau, Kant and Wollstonecraft concerned themselves with theories on femininity by attempting to describe "natural" characteristics specific to women. The description of such characteristics was meant to define a woman's role in a male-female relationship and in culture as a whole. It was used to try to settle the question of what type of education would be suitable for women to prepare them for marriage (Rousseau and Kant) or life in general (Wollstonecraft). In this discussion, the nature-culture issue plays a prominent role. Can one speak about an "authentic" female nature? What influence does culture have on it? What are the ideal cultural norms within which feminine nature can develop to the fullest? We shall see that Wollstonecraft draws conclusions very different from those drawn by Rousseau and Kant.

In the 19th century, a mosaic of views on women emerged. In this period, the feminist movement fought for issues such as the universal right to education, the vote and an independent legal status for women. These rights had seemed to be promised but not granted in the wake of the French Revolution. Philosophers differed in their reactions to the suffragist movement. Some saw the good sense of the struggle, others, such as Nietzsche and Schopenhauer reacted negatively to something so "unnatural". In the 19th century debate, the issues concerning the nature of women and their role in society became more emotionally charged than ever, appearing as they did within the context of a struggle for liberation. It is in this light that I shall discuss the views of Nietzsche and Schopenhauer in chapter eight.

In the first half of the 20th century, it seemed as though not much had changed in philosophy as a result of the 19th century women's liberation movement. A number of philosophers such as Buytendijk and de Beauvoir did indeed take up the philosophical issue of the nature of women and their role in society, but many of those who are considered to be the most prominent philosophers of those years took to a strategy of ignoring women's issues. A long list of such philosophers could be compiled. It would include one of the most important philosophers of this century, Martin Heidegger. Jacques Derrida, in his book *Spurs*, describes the way in which Heidegger responds to Nietzsche's idea of "woman as truth":

Heidegger quotes this sequence, even respects its underlining, but in his commentary (as seems to be generally the case) he skirts the woman, he abandons her there. Much as one might skip over a sensible image in a philosophy book or tear out an illustrated leaf or allegorical representation in a more serious volume, Heidegger analyses all the elements of Nietzsche's text with the sole exception of the idea's becoming-female (*sie wird Weib*). In such a way does one permit oneself to see without reading, to read without seeing.[1]

If there really are philosophers in our century who "read without seeing", this has fortunately proven to be more than compensated by women themselves. The second feminist wave, a movement generally dated as beginning in the 1960's, took up anew and expanded on the women's issues first raised in the 19th century. The results of this movement have become increasingly apparent in our society. One consequence of this influence is the volume of philosophical and other literature on women. More works concerning women have been written in our century than have ever appeared in the past. In philosophy, the number of studies appearing is overwhelming and makes any conscientious author ponder the advisability of adding more to this massive outpouring.

The feminist contribution to 20th century philosophical literature has, I think, two notable characteristics. Firstly, the literature is motivated by the desire for the liberation of women. In this sense, personal and ethical commitments and goals underly women's studies in philosophy. Secondly, it is new, because women, thanks to their access to higher education, have now read the philosophers of the past for themselves and react to them from out of their own experience of being women. Women reacted to the male philosophers who wrote about them in previous centuries, but never has the response been so scholarly and widespread. In the final chapter of this book, on Luce Irigaray, the emphasis will be on the struggle of women for recognition, or to use a more abstract philosophical phrase, on thinking from out of female subjectivity. By this I mean the desire of women to have their own voice, perspective, and critique of life and philosophy, to express their own identity as women and to declare their right to be what they want to be, to say what they want to say, beyond domination.

In constructing this book, I have not limited myself to a history of views of women presented by male philosophers but I have tried to present a dialogue between the two genders. The book starts with the views of Pythagorean women. Christine de Pizan's critique of the sexism of the later Middle Ages is discussed. The overview of classical modern thought includes the reaction of Mary Wollstonecraft to what she considers a lack of rationality in the view of women by men who considered reason to be the highest ideal. The book ends with Luce Irigaray's rethinking of female subjectivity. In this way, some skirmishes in the battle of the sexes are described in a historical context. Perhaps one will react to this announcement by thinking that this book will not present a dialogue but a free-for-all. And perhaps the suspicion will arise that the author, being female, is setting the odds. But that is not really the intention.

Much philosophical and other dialogue on male and female has, I think, caused misunderstandings between the sexes. Some male philosophers are nervous or even feel threatened about being confronted with historical research which they fear will only bring to the surface backward ideas which discredit philosophy and philosophers. Others consider this type of research to be the hobby of their female colleagues, not particularly worth taking note of or to be seen as academically respectable. Still others think of work in women's studies as monopolised by radical feminists who, because they are doing ideologically coloured work, are not to be taken seriously.

On the other side of the gender gap, some feminist writers have given the field a threatening aura by venting their anger and frustration at ideas they consider to be unacceptable. Such emotion can lead to the breathless announcement of the discovery of new horrors, the one-sided analysis of philosophical theories, or to a lack of appreciation for historical contexts. There is no lack of emotion in the area of women's studies and emotion often serves to cloud what should ultimately be an open discussion of the issues involved.

Therefore, this book is meant as an invitation to the reader to debate and weigh different views. Within the area of women's studies, philosophical questions are raised as to human nature, values and norms, and it seems to me that it is both inadvisable and impossible to lay down absolute criteria for these matters or to come to definitive conclusions concerning them. I doubt whether any one perspective on these questions is acceptable or correct for all people at all times. History warns us that the views on women in the history of philosophy and even in the relatively short period of the past twenty years have continually shifted due to all sorts of factors: religious, cultural, intellectual, social, and economic. But even though views change in the course of time, it

is also the philosophical task to rule out ideas which go against fundamental ethical notions of how we should speak of and deal with our
fellow human beings.

These considerations make the area of women's studies a delicate
one. There is the obligation to do justice to the history of philosophy
and to answer the traditional question of what truths can still be learned
from that history. But there is also the obligation to present an analysis
and critique of views which seem to violate fundamental principles and
values concerning right and wrong. As an author, I can only give
information and try to set a tone, for better or worse. I think this book
will only be meaningful if people react to what is being said and decide
for themselves how they wish to think about the issues being raised.

Finally, I would also like to make some short remarks on the two
terms, image and history, which appear in the subtitle of this book. The
concept of "image" is an important human notion in the sense that
human beings are not simply what they are. People develop images of
themselves and of other people; images are created in society; art,
science, literature, and philosophy are areas in which images of people
play a role. Images serve to tell people who they are and what they should
be. Very generally speaking, people not only have their own nature or
character, but also the capacity to alter themselves according to an
image, thus creating and re-creating themselves.

An image of certain people created by a philosopher can be thought
of as a "picture", but it is not always clear how well that picture reflects
their nature. This is part of the more general philosophical question of
whether or not philosophy is capable of presenting a "mirror" of nature
or reality.[2] Traditionally, philosophers believe that theoretical thought
is seeing with the mind's eye. They believe that when a mirror is flat
and smooth, a true image appears on it. In contemporary discussions,
the question has arisen of whether or not philosophy, thought or reason
can be considered to be mirroring reality. Are there perhaps quite
fundamental things wrong with such an idea?

There are two possible answers to this question with respect to the
creation of philosophically or theoretically based images of women.
Firstly, one can argue that the mirrors held up by male philosophers to
women are *a apriori* unreliable. The contemporary French philosopher
Luce Irigaray places the problem of the male origin and use of the
philosophical concept of the mirror at the center of her discussion of

images of men and women in western thought.[3] A mirror, Irigaray notes, reflects the person looking into it and the people looking into mirrors have mostly been men. In other words, the mirror as thought or philosophical thought is a product which may be reflecting only itself. Thus men create an image of women, an image which is a weak reflection of themselves and of their own thought. Women are described as "other" than men, as differing from the norm which they represent. Irigaray suggests that she would purposefully like to see women undermine the traditional idea of the mirror by making themselves into mirrors, cloudy or curved, concave or convex, thus taking away the illusion that there is one clear and "neutral" analysis possible of women on the basis of reason. A concave mirror can reflect light in such a way that it can burn an object placed in front of it. Symbolically, it can burn the person looking into it. A convex mirror distorts the person looking into it, turning the image into the ridiculous. In this way, the mirror is turned against the person wanting to look into it, undermining the whole concept of mirrors and mirroring in the traditional sense. This can be translated as a call to women to undermine the entire idea of philosophy as a field in which reason reigns supreme.

Secondly, one can in principle accept the idea of thought as mirroring reality and try to make the mirrors of philosophers more flat and smooth by clearing up the distortions which occur in them. Distortions can occur when there are prejudices in our culture concerning the nature and capacities of women, prejudices which do not give women a clear image of themselves, but serve to distort that self-image. Even idealised images of women can distort their nature and capacities as they and others see them. On this reading of the task of philosophy, the aim is not, as in the first example, to undermine a hopelessly prejudiced rationality but it is to clear up and sweep away prejudices.

However one evaluates the need for and status of mirrors and the accuracy of images presented to women in our western culture, the fact remains that the greatest power of an image is not so much that it describes someone but that it presents women with an ideal for which they must strive. For human beings, ideals are very compelling concepts which can (be used to) structure human lives or which can be the trigger for angry critique or rebellion.

The second term is that of history. A considerable number of studies have been written concerning the history and development of images of women in our culture. But why history, and what would be clarified by asking what the history of philosophy says about women? One of the most difficult questions which arises when examining the history of philosophers' theories about women is how to evaluate such theories in light of the culture in which they arose. Repeatedly, the question is asked in this book what this relationship is. Does philosophical discourse about women reflect the factual situation in a culture? Are philosophers on the whole eccentrics who present ideas which the majority of their contemporaries find strange? Do philosophers tend to write about matters which they disagree with and must we therefore read their theories on women as the search for ideals? In this book, we shall see that all these possibilities can occur. It is, however, important to be careful about drawing conclusions too rapidly on the difficult point of the relationship between philosophy and culture. It is not the case that the history of western philosophy can simply be seen as identical to the history of western culture. On the other hand, a study of the history of philosophy would lose all interest and meaning if philosophy were not very closely associated with its cultural context.

The history of philosophy is of importance and of interest not only for its relationship to culture, but also for itself, for its own developments and changes. Philosophical research also increases our knowledge and insight into our intellectual heritage as a whole. A historical study is guided by the leading intuition that we can learn from the past in our present situation and in the future. An investigation into the history of male and female images in philosophy can account for the occurrence of similar types of images in contemporary philosophy or culture as a whole. Here the question can be asked as to whether or not the creation and development of images of men and women can be wholly described as a historical-cultural process or whether it has an a-historical dimension. I will return to this issue in the conclusion of this book.

Knowledge of the history of philosophy is also a precondition for the possibility of ideology critique. When looking historically at images of women, it becomes clear that there are powerful ideologies concerning women. These ideologies in philosophy and culture have up to now been primarily created by males. Perhaps what is necessary now is the creation of a "critique of male thought". By looking at the history of how men spoke about women and the feminine in general, one can try to analyse characteristics of male thinking. Concerns with history can thus vary from a purely historical interest to a quite fundamental investigation of human thinking and reasoning processes.

Notes

1 J. Derrida, *Spurs/Éperons. Nietzsche's Styles/Les Styles de Nietzsche.* transl. by B. Harlow. Chicago/London, University of Chicago Press, 1978, p. 85. Derrida gives a detailed reading of Heidegger's view on gender in "Geschlecht. Différence sexuelle, différence ontologique" and "La main de Heidegger. (Geschlecht II)" in: J. Derrida, *Psyché. Inventions de l'autre.* Paris, Galilée, 1987, p. 395-451.

2 This issue is discussed at length in R. Rorty, *Philosophy and the Mirror of Nature.* New Jersey, Princeton University Press, 1979.

3 L. Irigaray, *Speculum. Of the Other Woman.* transl. by Gillian C. Gill. Ithaca, New York, Cornell University Press, 1985.

1   The Pythagorean School

1   Introduction

I would like to begin this book by focussing on the most primordial image of male and female which has been repeated throughout history and which has had an especially strong hold on the human imagination. By this primordial image, I mean seeing women mainly in terms of their domestic roles as daughters, wives, mothers and grandmothers, whose main source of self-identification and purpose in life lies in the realm of reproduction and the family or the realm of the "natural". Men are traditionally seen as finding their identity and activities outside the sphere of the home, in the workforce, warfare, government, the public interest, and providing for and protecting the family, realms of the "cultural". The man is seen as returning to the home from out of the public sphere, and when at home is considered, in legal and personal terms, the head of the household. Such a social order, the most pervasive one on earth, is called patriarchal because the power and status of women within the home is considered to be lesser than that of men both inside the home and outside it.

Most if not all images of men and women serve to justify, confirm or criticise this basic social order. This order is also the point of departure of most philosophical analyses of women in western society, analyses which attempt to either confirm or deny the legitimacy of the patriarchal order. In feminist literature and philosophy there is a search for redescriptions of the nature and social roles of women. Examples are the re-examination of the history of patriarchy; attempts to find evidence of non-patriarchal cultures or pre-patriarchal matriarchies; the search for images of women which emphasise the talents and strengths of women outside of the home; calls for women to liberate themselves from their domestic roles in order to realise their potential in the public realm. The patriarchal order is seen as working with negative images or taboos in order to strengthen its hold on people, excluding or even demonising women who do not fit in or who do not wish to fit into it. Feminist critiques of the patriarchal order thus include attempts to rehabilitate non-domestic images of women, all the way to those of the woman as witch or goddess. Feminism maintains that the patriarchal order has always "placed" or "identified" women in a manner which is reduction-istic, hierarchical, and that it denies them of their possibilities and talents.

In this first chapter, I would like to look at the historical question of the emergence of patriarchy from two perspectives. I will first describe one of the oldest known concepts of a patriarchal order in the history of philosophy in order to show that male-female imagery as we know it today is not a result, as has sometimes been argued, of the development of the nuclear family but was already theoretically well in place in the 6th century B.C. and may in fact be as old as mankind itself. In the second part of the chapter, I will consider what some philosophers have said about the historical emergence of patriarchy: when did it develop? why did it develop?

2   The Pythagorean Letters and Fragments

The Pythagorean school, founded by Pythagoras in the 6th century B.C., is one of the oldest schools of philosophy in the Greek-Western tradi-tion. Interest has been shown in this school in women's studies because of two ways in which the Pythagoreans describe women: one on the metaphysical level and the other on the everyday level. Common to both types of approach is the Pythagorean point of departure in a philosophy which sees the world in terms of order, harmony and mathematically describable relationships. The question is how women are placed in this order and how they are evaluated in terms of it.

On the first and more primary level, the Pythagorean school made one of the first known attempts to create a metaphysics which includes the categories male and female. This was done by means of an opposi-tion table in which male-female is one of the fundamental categories of reality. There were ten such contrasts in the table: limit/unlimited, even/odd, one/many, right/left, male/female, rest/motion, straight/curved, light/dark, good/bad, square/oblong. From this table it can be seen that the female is on the negative side, the male on the positive. The "logic" behind such a categorisation is that elements which are "good", "ordered", and "harmonious", are "rational" and positive, their opposites negative.[1] Women seem to be placed in the category which includes the irrational and inferior. Such a metaphysics is surprising:

why would anyone want to make the male-female distinction into a fundamental category of reality and place the female on the negative, irrational side? One can speculate that perhaps men think women are less rational then they are because men and women think differently; or that perhaps at that time there was already a difference in the amount of formal, theoretical, education which men and women had; or perhaps that it is simply the desire of men to see themselves as superior to women, with superiority linked to rationality and intelligence. This type of theory formation can also be seen as being embedded in, and having implications for, social contexts. On the metaphysical plane, women are placed on a secondary level, excluded from the the highest, positive, realm. Their lack of status in this realm can be linked to their confinement to the home, to their domestic education, and to the broader aim of keeping women in their own sphere through the confirmation of the superiority of the male in his realm. In short, it can be argued that this metaphysics is tied in with patriarchal notions.

Besides describing the place of the female on the metaphysical level, the Pythagoreans also had views on the nature and roles of women in everyday life. Women were to be trained to develop their capacities, including those of rationality and judgment, within the home. On this level, one can see an earnest desire to appreciate women and to help them develop themselves so that they can function as well as possible in this realm. However, besides strengthening the family structure by encouraging women to develop the skills they need to run a home, the training and advice serves male interests. As Jean-Jacques Rousseau was to remark many centuries later, no husband or male philosopher, however much he wishes to confirm his own position in the public realm, wants an irrational, uninteresting or hopeless woman as wife and mother.

The Pythagorean texts which speak of the roles of women in the domestic sphere are more than 2,000 years old. They consist of fragments of letters and books of advice written (or so it is claimed) by female philosophers for other women. It is thought that Pythagoras (born circa 570 B.C.), the founder of the school bearing his name, encouraged women to apply the principles of his philosophy to their own situations and to questions as to their nature, their virtues and how to comport themselves. The texts are called "economic" writings because they deal with the *oikos*, that is, the realm of the home. They are *pseudepigrapha,* pseudonymous writings. Attempts have been made to trace the identity of the authors to whom the texts were attributed in ancient times and to determine if they were indeed written by the women cited as their authors.[2] The texts as a whole are dated within the following three categories: early Pythagorean, dating from the end of the 6th century B.C. to the end of the 4th century B.C.; late Pythagorean, from about 425 B.C. to about 100 A.D.; neo-Pythagorean of the Hellenistic period, dating from the 1st century B.C. to the 3rd century A.D.[3]

Despite their age, we can readily recognise the patterns in which women are spoken about in these texts. The writers of these letters and fragments confirm a patriarchal social structure: the main purpose of life for women lies in the realm of reproduction and the family. Women are placed squarely within the domestic sphere and the focus of the authors is on the virtues to be realised in it. The first duty of a woman is towards her family: her parents, husband, children and household, which in this time and culture means an extended household of slaves and guests. Everything in this sphere must be well run. Basically, everyone must be kept happy and handled in such a fashion that all the members of the household will live productive, good and, for the freemen, comfortable lives. The husband, children and slaves must all be approached in a manner appropriate to them: the husband respected, the children not spoiled and the slaves kept at work. The virtues women must have are those of moderation, harmony, strength of character, modesty, practical sense, with, both for themselves and in terms of how they treat the children, a tinge of asceticism. Besides leading to good management of the household and expressing philosophical-ethical ideals, the virtues are seen as ensuring the best possible life for the woman practising them, ultimately aiding the person following the instructions to attain the greatest possible happiness through right behaviour.[4]

The virtues relate not only to the individual and her family, but also to various broader human contexts within which women live. Behaviour connects to social, legal and religious spheres. Women should follow the laws of the land; the gods will punish unvirtuous behaviour; other people, such as members of one's household and friends, are dependent on the virtuous behaviour and wisdom of women; social mores demand that one have a good name in society, something which is important because it strengthens the social life and position of the family. The mention of these contexts serves to emphasise the importance of the virtues being advocated and also gives them an element of pressure. Women are reminded that society and the gods are watching them and that there is more to win or lose by their behaviour than the ordering of relationships within the family itself.[5]

The texts have a strongly conservative flavour which may appeal to "traditionalists" even today. There are, however, some assumptions made and some advice given which mark these texts as a reflection of their culture. For example, the Greek notion of confining women to the home during the day is mentioned in these texts. The reason for such a practice was to ensure that the woman's reputation was not sullied. The virtuous woman, faithful to her husband, only goes out briefly with her servants to go shopping and leaves the home only towards nightfall in order to go to the temple to pray. Because the ideal woman places all her worth in marriage, she not only serves and obeys her husband, but if necessary accepts the sexual double standard that "a man is forgiven his transgression, a woman not", not only by society, but also by the gods.[6] Keeping the peace at home is all-important, so that if her husband does have an affair, she is to say nothing about it and be assured that it is only a temporary thing. Besides, a woman is counselled, if she complains she will only make matters worse and sour her own life. To keep the peace, a woman must always share her husband's opinions and keep up the appearance of a harmonious household.[7] I think that behind this advice which may even go too far for present-day traditionalists, the fundamental presupposition of the texts is universal in its appeal: the idea that certain attitudes and virtues will lead to more happiness or good than others.

The concept of ideals and with it the notion of self-fulfillment and happiness is not a naïve one: the two opposing sides in this debate whom we can roughly call traditionalists versus feminists both believe in these things. Taking the side of the more traditional intrepretation of the self-fulfillment of women, one can argue that people in many societies throughout the ages have thought that a woman's happiness and fulfillment can be found in the domestic realm. The Pythagorean texts are, moreover, more subtle than many others on this topic because there is an awareness in these texts that there will probably always be a gap between the ideal of domestic happiness and reality. Perhaps this insight into this gap even lies at the basis of the letters on the same fundamental level as the ideal of goodness and happiness: why else write this advice, give these admonitions? The texts are quite clear in their view of virtue and happiness in the domestic realm as something which is not simply given, but as something which must be fought for. The authors warn that even when women aim to be virtuous, there is a risk that the household will not function well, the children be spoiled, one's reputation tarnished, and that one's husband takes up with a courtesan. Virtue and the following of good advice will minimize these risks, yet at times the only realistic goal may be that of damage containment.

Finally, in evaluating the relationship between these texts and reality, one can ask if the principles recommended by the Pythagorean texts reflect everyday life in the upper classes of ancient Greece. Or did they reflect the principles of those people who followed the Pythagorean school of philosophy? Or is all this advice not a reflection of how things were but an attempt to put people back on what was considered to be the right track?

3   The History of Patriarchy

Even though the philosophical texts written by the Pythagoreans by no means take us back to the dawn of time, it is striking that the patriarchal order described in these texts is so recognisable even to "modern" people today. From a philosophical point of view, this observation raises a number of questions as to the origin, tenacity, power and legitimacy of the patriarchal order. A great deal of research has been done in fields such as history and cultural anthropology to trace the nature and origin of patriarchy. Philosophers have also tried to account for the deep historical roots and power of patriarchy. I would like to give several examples of how they explain the emergence and power of patriarchy.

Plato, in the *Menexenus*, gives a (pre)-historical account of the emergence of the patriarchal order. The *Menexenus* is an account by Socrates of a "Remembrance Day" speech he heard being given in Athens by Aspasia, the wife of Pericles. It opens with a glorifying, celebratory account of the history of Greece and Athens. Aspasia begins by telling about the origin of Greece. She states that the motherhood of the land of Attica is the source of everything: the earth is the primary nurturing mother. It precedes and is an example for human motherhood. Human mothers, in bringing forth children and caring for them, imitate the earth. The earthly, biological, nurturing, and domestic realms are seen to be basic to the development of human society in Greece. The first order is therefore a feminine one. The emergence of the state is a male innovation and achievement. With the creation of the state, different forms of government come into being. Aspasia mentions aristocracy, democracy, monarchy, and oligarchy. As a result of this political order, the Athenian "fathers and brethern...did both in their public and private capacity many noble deeds famous over the whole world".[8] The female origins of the land and the family as well as their value are turned into the basis of male achievements in the public realm on which the new focus comes.

The idea that the emergence of the patriarchal order is associated with the development of a certain sociology is basic to Plato's account and is widespread among philosophers. The family structure, with the woman in the home caring for the biological unit, emerges as a distinct entity when society begins to distinguish between the private and the public, the family and the state, personal ethics and a political-legal system. Plato of course did not like the public-private distinction nor individual family units. He presents his alternative to these structures in the *Republic.*

Aristotle sees social roles as the fundamental reason for the emergence of the family unit and the role of women in that unit. He sees the family as the basis for the stability, order and wealth of society. He argues that without the family unit as a basic element in society, the state cannot function. In his view, the creation of a traditional family unit has two origins: in the natural tendencies of people and in the pragmatic needs of people and society as a whole. Aristotle thinks it is important to do all we can to maintain a strong family structure in society.[9]

Hegel, in his great work *The Phenomenology of Spirit* also presents an account of the emergence of patriarchy as the development of a division between the realms of the family and the state, a separation which results in different areas of competence for the feminine and the masculine. Hegel's inspiration for these ideas is an ancient Greek source, Sophocles' *Antigone.* Sophocles' *Antigone* is a tragedy and Hegel sees the first emergence of the the state as a onesided and hence tragic (in the literal meaning of this word) event. Hegel's view, resembling that of Plato's *Menexenus,* is that the primary reality is a feminine, natural,

familial, order which is replaced in dominance by a masculine order
whose main characteristic is the creation of human law. Hegel sees the
emergence of the masculine order as a tragic conflict situation because
it arises out of a conflict between the realm of the family, in which the
laws are based on the commands of the household gods, and the realm
of the state where human laws are to be followed. The state, in order to
assert itself, must in fact defeat the moral rules of the familial order and
its gods. Hegel sees the primordial example of this conflict in the tragic
confrontation between a woman, Antigone, and a man, King Creon.
Antigone wishes to follow the laws of the family and the gods of the
underworld in her desire to bury her deceased brother Polyneices. Her
desire, however, stands in stark conflict to the decree of Creon that
Polyneices is not to receive a decent burial because he died as a traitor
to the state. Both Antigone and Creon are confronted with tragedy:
Antigone, because she will not recognise the legitimacy of the legal order
of the state, dies at the hand of that state; Creon, because he has defied
the gods of the underworld, is punished as well. For Hegel, this story is
an illustration of what he calls the birth of the ethical order. Ultimately,
the aim of society is to overcome the onesidedness of the conflicts of
interest between the natural laws which govern the family and the legal
order of the state. Only when the family functions harmoniously within
the political and legal order will the tragic conflict be resolved. But
despite Hegel's optimism that the tragedy which lies at the birth of the
division between the family and the state will be overcome, he also sees
the relationship between these two units as one of perpetual strife. The
family is a biological unit, meant to produce and maintain life. The
state, on the other hand, in order to assert its power and legitimacy, will
in the end always demand the ultimate obedience from its citizens: the
willingness to sacrifice loyalty to the family in favour of loyalty to the
state. This conflict returns again and again when the state demands the
ultimate biological sacrifice: the willingness to die for it. Women will
always want to protect and keep their husbands and sons. Therefore,
Hegel states that the feminine will always try to undermine the authority
of the state. Woman is, he says, "the irony" of the state.[10]

   Plato and Hegel see the state and hence patriarchy as emerging from
a separation which occurs when the biological order becomes dominated
by the legal order. A quite different view is presented by J.-J. Rousseau,
whose point of departure is that of "natural" evolution. Rousseau claims

that it is not the familial order which is historically basic but simply the fact of reproduction. Men and women in the beginning merely met for the purpose of conception; the woman drove the man away when she had conceived and raised the children on her own. The family structure emerges when a certain role division is discovered to be convenient. At that point, the division arises between the male as hunter and protector of the family and the woman as caring for the home, the male and their children. This role division makes use of the "natural" strengths of the two genders and is a better means for meeting the needs of all concerned. Out of this order, the social and legal order arises. Rousseau, unlike Hegel, does not see this development as progress. For Rousseau, every social structure which humans create removes them a step from their "natural" origins and condition.

Within many religious philosophical traditions, such as in the view of St. Thomas Aquinas, role divisions and the structure of the family do not have a social or biological history, but are divinely decreed, part of the ordering of creation. The roles which women have in the domestic realm are then justified, as they were by the Pythagoreans, on the basis of divine ordinance.

I have given some examples of philosophical accounts of the emergence of patriarchy, some of which are taken from the works of philosophers who will be discussed in more detail in later chapters. This brief survey shows that there are various ways in which to account for the emergence and power of the patriarchal order. Alternatively, one can also conclude that the patriarchal order is all of the above: a sociological phenomenon based on a complex private-public ordering of human life; the domination of a male ruling order over a female biological order; a convenient solution to the needs of people living in private and public structures; a role division which takes advantage of differing capacities of male and female; and a reflection of a "natural desire" which people manifest in this ordering.

4   Conclusions

These theories on the origin of patriarchy and the fact that patriarchy is so widespread makes the drawing of conclusions about the Pythagorean texts particularly difficult. What is "good" and what is "bad" about them? Do we have any right to judge them at all, even if the intention of such a judgment is to raise awareness of the rights of women to be themselves and not be stifled by an order placed over them? Or do women themselves help form and maintain this order because they feel comfortable in "their own" realm? Do the virtues women are being urged to develop serve the interests of women or the social context to which they are being referred? Is this the way women themselves want to be or are these ideals imposed on them "from outside"? Will following the precepts of the Pythagorean school truly ensure the happiness and self-fulfilment of women? Perhaps the only way to deal fairly with these texts and their historical context is to mention the various ways one can react to them.

Waithe, in her commentary on these texts, argues that they should be acceptable to feminists. After all, she argues, if it is really true that these texts were written by women, Pythagoras and the Pythagorean school accepted and encouraged women philosophers and had respect for the capacity of women to understand these teachings, an emancipatory idea. Furthermore, she argues, the virtues spoken about demand a great deal of women, thus showing respect for their strength of character and the high ideals which they are capable of attaining.[11] Another possible approach to the texts is to take the line of Elshtain.[12] Elshtain argues that a very basic category of non-emancipatory thought about women is the public-private distinction, that is, placing women within the sphere of the private, men in the sphere of the public. As long as women are seen as functioning exclusively within the realm of the private, no matter how well and according to whatever ideals, it means that they are excluded from the public realm and from the privileges which functioning in the public realm entails. A third option is to say that feminism should not prescribe the interpretation of the texts or to judge the values and roles which are being assigned to these women. In other words, feminism should be open to all forms of life for women as long as women themselves have freely chosen to live that way. Finally, one can also approach the texts by comparing the ethical standards and values they propose with those that apply in our culture today. Seen in this light, some of the virtues and values mentioned by the texts may be considered to be acceptable, others not, and one can argue for and against specific points raised.

The Pythagorean texts show how fundamental and ancient a certain view of women is: of women in the home, self-sacrificing, virtuous, supporting order and family values. In the next chapter, however, a very different view on women will be presented in light of the philosophy of Plato.

Notes

1   G. Lloyd, *The Man of Reason. "Male" and "Female" in Western Philosophy.* London, Methuen, 1984, p. 3. Lloyd opens her book with mention of the Pythagorean table of opposites, arguing that the Pythagoreans are typical of the entire western philosophical tradition in excluding women from rationality.

2   For a detailed discussion of these technical philological matters, see: Holger Thesleff, *An Introduction to the Pythagorean Writings of the Hellenistic Period.* Acta Academiae Aboensis xxiv.3. Abo, 1961, p. 7-23 and p. 30-85. See also: M.E. Waithe, ed. *A History of Women Philosophers. Vol. 1, 600 b.c. – 500 a.d.* Dordrecht/London/Lancaster, Martinus Nijhoff, 1987. Chapter 4, "Authenticating the Fragments and Letters", by M.E. Waithe and Vicki Lynn Harper, p. 59-74.

3   M.E. Waithe, *A History of Women Philosophers. Vol. 1, 600 b.c. – 500 a.d.* Dordrecht, London, Lancaster, Martinus Nijhoff, 1987, p. 11.

4   M.E. Waithe, *A History of Women Philosophers. Vol. 1, 600 b.c. – 500 a.d.* Dordrecht, London, Lancaster, Martinus Nijhoff, 1987, p. 47-48.

5   M.E. Waithe, *A History of Women Philosophers. Vol. 1, 600 b.c. – 500 a.d.* Dordrecht, London, Lancaster, Martinus Nijhoff, 1987, p. 30-31, 47-48.

6   M.E. Waithe, *A History of Women Philosophers. Vol. 1, 600 b.c. – 500 a.d.* Dordrecht, Lancaster, London, Martinus Nijhoff, 1987, p. 26-26, 44-46.

7   M.E. Waithe, *A History of Women Philosophers. Vol. 1, 600 b.c. – 500 a.d.* Dordrecht, Lancaster, London, Martinus Nijhoff, 1987, p. 32-34, 46.

8   Plato, *Collected Dialogues.* transl. by Hamilton and Cairns. Princeton, Princeton University Press, 1973, p. 189-191. *Menexenus* 237d-239c.

9   I will discuss Plato's and Aristotle's view of the family and the state in more detail in chapters two and three and will show how their views differ.

10 G.F.W. Hegel, *Phenomenology of Spirit.* transl. by A.V. Miller. Oxford, Oxford University Press, 1977, p. 279-289. (A. The True Spirit. The Ethical Order, paragraph 444-476). See also: L. Irigaray, *Speculum. De l'autre femme.* Paris, Minuit, 1974; L. Irigary, *Éthique de la différence sexuelle.* Rotterdam, Centrale Interfaculteit Erasmus

University, 1983, p. 1-26; and R. van Riessen, *Antigone's Bruidsvertrek. De plaats van de Antigone in Hegel's denken over de vrouw.* Kampen, Kok, 1986.

11 M.E. Waithe, *A History of Women Philosophers. Vol. I,* 600 *B.C.* – 500 *A.D.* Dordrecht, London, Lancaster, Martinus Nijhoff, 1987, p. 25.

12 J.B. Elshtain, *Public Man, Private Woman: Women in Social and Political Thought.* Princeton, Princeton University Press, 1981.

2 Images of Women in Plato

1 Introduction

Plato (c. 429-347 B.C.) is generally considered to be the first and most influential philosopher in the western tradition. Plato does not present us with a systematic view of women, but with a somewhat mixed set of ideas. This mixture can be partly due to the incidental nature of references to women within his dialogues and partly to the fact that he may not have been concerned with presenting a complete systematic view on this issue in the modern sense of the word. The reading of Plato's views becomes more complex because the main speaker in the dialogues is not Plato himself but Socrates and Socrates often speaks ironically. Socrates is sometimes also ambiguous when speaking about women, making a straightforward interpretation difficult.

First, I will contrast Socrates' view of women and marriage to that of the writers of the Pythagorean school discussed in the previous chapter. I will do so by describing three women in Socrates' life: Xanthippe, Aspasia and Diotima. Secondly, I will describe Plato's view of the role of women in his ideal state. The picture he presents in the *Republic* of the nature of women, the family and division of labour between men and women is quite revolutionary and is the source of considerable criticism by Aristotle, a critique discussed in the next chapter.

2 Xanthippe

Perhaps the most famous and very un-Pythagorean marriage of ancient Greece was that between Socrates and Xanthippe. Socrates (469-399 B.C.) is believed to have married Xanthippe when he was around fifty years old. He may have married her in order to have children, a common convention in his culture and time. Ultimately, the couple had three children, most likely born when Socrates was in his fifties and sixties.

The marriage was stormy. No doubt both partners were at fault. Socrates himself relates in the *Apology* that he did not have time to earn a living as other men did because of his philosophizing. The result was that, despite being invited to dinner parties by wealthy friends, he was quite poor. The poverty in which Xanthippe had to raise her children as well as the philosophical work of Socrates, which had him going out a great deal, may have caused tensions. But Socrates also felt attracted to young men and defended homosexual love as part of the education of younger men. It is difficult to estimate the cultural factors in this bisexuality. On the one hand, it seems a more common phenomenon in ancient Greece than in many other societies, yet on the other hand, the Pythagorean texts which we looked at in the previous chapter do not mention this particular risk to the well-being of wives. In any case, some or all of these factors may have caused difficulties between Socrates and Xanthippe.

Also in contrast to the harmonious Pythagorean attitude which women are advised to have to marital problems, Xanthipppe was known as a woman who did not hide her emotions or mince words. Xenophon in his *Symposium* characterises Xanthippe as the most furious and angry woman up to his time (400 B.C.) and most likely of all future generations. A famous account of a marital fight is as follows. Socrates leaves the house after a fight; he suddenly finds himself deluged by a tub of wash water, poured on him by Xanthippe from a second story window. Socrates remarks that after the thunder comes the rain. The image here seems to be one of Socrates suffering through the marriage stoically, Xanthippe with a great deal of frustration.[1]

The most poignant description of Xanthippe is given in the *Phaedo* at the scene of Socrates' death.[2] Xanthippe comes with the children to bid her husband farewell. She is taken out of the room crying, for otherwise her emotions would interfere with Socrates' desire for a final conversation with his friends and with his plan to die in a stoical, dignified manner. The passage has some ironic overtones. As she leaves, Xanthippe says that the men will now have their last conversation. In the text, the comment is made that this is typically the remark of a woman. The remark could be seen as typical of a woman because of the preconception that women tend to comment on the obvious. The reaction can also be interpreted as typical of Xanthippe. If this is what is meant and if we can believe the accounts of her character, the comment must have been made in an aggressive or sarcastic way, in the sense of "go ahead, you can have your conversation now". If this is the case, Xanthippe demonstrates that she sees very clearly that the situation is one of her own exclusion.

As Xanthippe predicts, the men indeed have their conversation, but in the end the men all end up crying as well, with one also being sent away. The comment is made in the text that it is shameful that the men end up crying. That was precisely the reason the women were sent away. It is to Plato's credit that he paints a very true picture, one which goes beyond the stereotypes of male and female: despite all the ideals, men too are capable of losing control. Yet Plato does not take the further step of saying that it may be a good thing for men to show their emotions. That would go against the stoical and dignified ideals of manhood.

If one may believe the 19th century German philosopher Friedrich Nietzsche, Socrates' irony also extended to his own marriage. In a marvellous passage in the *Genealogy of Morals*, Nietzsche argues that a philosopher is a person who basically wants independence, not to be tied down by a woman, family and material worries. Such day-to-day concerns inhibit the philosopher from concentrating on higher things. Nietzsche calls this the ascetic ideal, an ideal which is ultimately aimed at attaining an optimal amount of concentration. Asceticism is the source of philosophical power because by means of it philosophers attempt to make reality fit into their own theoretical framework. This framework, removed from everyday reality, is imposed on others as the true reality. Therefore, asceticism ultimately aims at influencing others and the way they live their lives. It is, to use Nietzsche's words, a will to power. Nietzsche lists some philosophers who never married: Heraclitus, Plato, Descartes, Spinoza, Leibniz, Kant and Schopenhauer. He exclaims that one cannot even *imagine* them being married. But he states that Socrates is an exception because he married ironically just to demonstrate the fact that philosophers who marry belong in a comedy (one can think here of Sophocles' satirical comedy *The Clouds*), not in a serious context. Socrates, the philosopher of irony, *would* be the one who would want to prove by his own lifestyle the fact that philosophers should not marry.[3]

All this is quite removed from the Pythagorean view in which the woman provides a comfortable support system for the functioning of the man. According to Nietzsche, philosophers need more space than marriage can give and some women, like Xanthippe, are not willing or able to agree to that.

3 Aspasia

Socrates also had a tendency to admire talented women who did not, as the Pythagoreans advised, simply keep to the home. This is shown by two examples, that of Aspasia and Diotima. The fact that we know of the existence of these two women indicates that in ancient Athenian society it was possible for women of a certain social, intellectual or spiritual standing to gain acceptance. But these two women have another curious characteristic in common: Socrates calls both of them his "teachers": Aspasia in rhetoric, Diotima in love. It is therefore interesting to see what Socrates' attitude towards them is.

Aspasia, a contemporary of Socrates, was first the mistress and later the wife of Pericles, the famous Athenian orator. It was said that she was so charming and beautiful that two wars were fought over her. Yet it seems, from rumours in Athens, that her marriage to Pericles was not entirely happy: she was said to keep women for him.[4]

At the beginning and end of the *Menexenus*, Socrates makes remarks about Aspasia and about a speech she gave the day before in Athens.[5] These remarks are full of irony and double meanings. On the one hand, Socrates says that he admires Aspasia. On the other hand, there is a joking atmosphere about his admiration. Double entendres and insinuations are mixed with expressions of admiration. Did she really write this speech herself? Did she take passages from the speeches of Pericles to make her speeches? Or was it the other way around: was she ghost writing speeches for Pericles? Is the speech Socrates tells about in the dialogue really her speech or is it Socrates' own satire on her speech? Stangely enough, the way in which Socrates speaks of Aspasia is somehow easily recognisable by women. Is the admiration for the achievements of women always sincere? Why do women often have the feeling that their accomplishments are relativized and in extreme cases minimalized? Are men uncomfortable with the achievements of women?

Apart from the male-female dynamics and perhaps a personal tension between Socrates and Aspasia which might be at the root of Socrates' ironic words, it is clear that he did not have a high regard for rhetoricians, especially not for those who appealed to nationalistic sentiments. In this sense, Socrates' target is more than Aspasia herself. She is being used as a prominent example of the rhetoricians with whom Socrates is not impressed. But why pick a woman, his "teacher", as the personification of the rhetoricians? Presumably because Aspasia was well-known and an easy target. Is this equal opportunity in the sense that Socrates does not distinguish between a man and a woman in his attack? Or is a woman more vulnerable to such an attack, having the additional characteristic of herself being an exception, as Menexenus notes? But the temptation of linking women and sophistry is surely one that Socrates could not resist.

4 Diotima

The third female character whom I would like to look at is Diotima. Diotima is the wise priestess whom Socrates calls his teacher in matters of love and appears in one of the most well-known of the Platonic dialogues, the *Symposium*, that is, the dinner party.

We know very little about the historical Diotima. It is likely that she indeed existed, since most of the characters in the dialogues of Plato were real historical figures.[6] When introducing her, Socrates calls her a woman from Mantinea, an expert on love. She came to Athens when people were sacrificing to the gods to avoid the plague and she managed to keep the plague away for ten years.

Plato's view of love says a great deal about his view of women, especially because he wishes to include and exclude them from certain aspects of love. To clarify this issue, I will discuss the question of the relationship between his view of love and his attitude to Diotima, a woman, who presents his theories.[7]

Diotima begins by defining eros as the desire to possess something forever. The first form in which eros is expressed is a feminine one, that is, through pregnancy and procreation. To want to have children is a godly desire, it is the yearning for immortality in mortals who want to pass something of themselves along which will reach beyond their own lives. Diotima says that reproduction occurs in beauty. A beautiful father and mother wish to produce a beautiful child, while ugliness does not reproduce and is not in harmony with the godly. The desire to have children in beauty is the expression of the urge of humans to have the immortality of the gods. This desire, says Diotima, is so strong that people and even animals are prepared to sacrifice everything, even their own lives, for their children. At this point, it would seem that Diotima's view of love says something positive about women and is in harmony with female values. According to traditional views, such as that of the Pythagoreans, physical reproduction is the realm of the feminine. Yet for Diotima, the level of physical reproduction is only a first and lower stage of the realisation of love. Her theory is hierarchical: she speaks of levels of increased abstraction. The more abstract the realisation of eros is, the more value it has.

The higher form of pregnancy is spiritual pregnancy. In spiritual creation, man continually forms new ideas, forgets old ones and transmits ideas through time. This desire is also a desire for eternity and immortality. People, here too, are ready to do practically anything to win eternal fame, to mark themselves as the authors of eternally preserved ideas. It is this type of longing, according to Diotima, which motivates authors, statesmen, sophists, heroes and philosophers, that is, people working in culture, arts and sciences. Those people who long for spiritual children prefer them to physical ones. The spiritual children are nobler and assure the author of even greater immortality. Diotima mentions Homer and Hesiod as examples of people who are immortal in the highest sense of the word.

Diotima also describes levels of abstraction in the objects of human love. She speaks of the progression from the love of a man for a woman, which lies on the level of physical reproduction, to the love of a man for another man, in which the spiritual side is of importance. Whether oriented to male or female, a person is first attracted to physical beauty and falls in love with one physical body. At the next stage, he will understand that one beautiful body is much like another beautiful body and he will fall in love with *all* beautiful bodies, leaving behind him the intense love he felt for the one beautiful body. But after the stage at which he desires all beautiful bodies, he will realise that a beautiful soul is much nobler than a beautiful body and he will love the beautiful soul even though it may live in a not-so-beautiful body. This level of love will make him appreciate the beauty of institutions and of the sciences. After that, he will turn to all the ways in which beauty manifests itself in the spiritual dimension and, by listening to discourses and discovering new ideas, he will be driven to long for all sorts of knowledge. This will lead him to appreciate beauty in the highest degree.

The final goal of love is to go beyond all these forms. It is to see love itself, as it really is, in a vision of the most exalted, eternal beauty. This vision goes beyond the oppositions which are part of the structure of love. It is the vision of beauty itself, one with itself, free from all limitations and constraints. As a result of seeing this beauty, man will also see true virtue and be in contact with truth. And, once having conceived and brought forth true virtue, this man will be able "to win the friendship of the gods".

Socrates' description of Diotima's ideas makes it apparent that her views differ from those of the Pythagorean women, sounding suspiciously Socratic and male. For Diotima, spiritual reproduction is higher than physical reproduction. Yet she must have realised that women in ancient Greece were seen primarily in terms of their capacity for physical reproduction, not for spiritual company. Homosexual love, according to Diotima, is a higher form of love than heterosexual love.[8] This view of relationships excludes women who have already been excluded from the educational process. Sexuality is made secondary to an intellectual relationship: the homo-sexuality she speaks of is perhaps better described as "homo-intellectuality". Such an interpretation would be consistent with Diotima's view that the highest form of love is something which makes the person turn away entirely from human relationships, to come to a higher, ultra-human form of self-identification. The contemporary philosopher L. Irigaray in her criticism of this Platonic notion says that the ultimate goal of "friendship with the gods" is actually a form of self-projection or self-aggrandisation.[9]

Women who see their purpose in life and their honour in terms of the home, physical reproduction, marriage, and heterosexuality have been placed on the lowest level of all. It is therefore all the more surprising that Diotima, a woman, is saying these things. One would expect Diotima to be supportive of other women. In her defence, it can be argued that Diotima is not speaking for herself. She is being quoted by Socrates on the occasion of a male dinner party which she could not, as a woman, attend. A problem in the interpretation of the work of Plato is that it is not always clear whose point of view is being expressed. This problem applies not only to the characters in the dialogues but also to the issue of how to distinguish between the views of Socrates and Plato.[10]

One possibility is that Socrates is telling the truth, that Diotima indeed taught these ideas. The other possibility is that what Diotima says are in fact Socrates' views and that he wants someone else to present them – and for some reason he wants that someone to be a woman.

Diotima, as a woman, is perhaps being used as the justification for
Socrates' views on love. Perhaps Socrates thinks that if a woman were
to express his views, they might seem to be more "objective", since
Diotima is not part of the male society attending the party. The effect
of that would be that her views would be seen to be true and relevant
for both genders, not just for the interested parties, the men. In a sense
that would be a back-handed compliment to women, implying that a
man would like a woman to agree with his idea of love. Alternatively,
it is possible that the men would have so little regard for a woman's view
on love that it is not the case that Diotima was introduced to give a
measure of objectivity or universality to Socrates' views. There is the
possibility that Diotima, as a priestess, is not really considered to be a
"woman" at all in the eyes of the ancient Greeks; perhaps only a married
woman is a "real woman". In that case, her role of priestess, representing
a higher form of wisdom, justifies the views in that they come from the
most "objective" level of all, someone who is neither male nor female
who represents the highest possible spiritual values.

From this short survey of the three most important women in
Socrates' life, we can conclude that they come across as less domesticated
than the women described by the Pythagoreans. We saw that the
Pythagorean women were not always completely happy in their roles.
The different lifestyle of Socrates' female friends does not seem to give
them perfect happiness either. Xanthippe struggled in a miserable
marriage, Aspasia's competence is questioned, and Diotima serves
Socrates' purposes.

5   Plato's View of Women in the Ideal State

In the *Republic*, Plato describes Socrates' view of the ideal social and
political structure of the state. Plato re-examines, among others, questions as to the nature of women and their roles in society, the division
of labour between the genders, and the family structure. Plato is known
for his call to do away with the traditional family structure and to liberate
women to fulfill all the roles in society of which they are capable,
unhindered by domestic cares. But how liberating is this side of Plato's
philosophy really?[11]

Fundamental to the discussion of the roles of male and female in the state is the concept of human nature. According to Plato, a human being's role in society must reflect the natural capacities of that person. This is because he takes as his point of departure the principle that "...to the same natures we must...assign the same pursuits".[12] He then asks: "...for what art or pursuit concerned with the conduct of a state the woman's nature differs from the man's".[13] The final answer to this question is slow in coming and along the way there seems to be some Socratic irony again. The first position which is considered is that "...the one sex is far surpassed by the other in everything, one may say. Many women, it is true, are better than many men in many things, but broadly speaking..." women are less strong and capable than men.[14] This idea is rejected and a jump is made to the final conclusion there are after all no *essential* differences between men and women in terms of their natures and their roles in society:

Then there is no pursuit of the administrators of a state that belongs to a woman because she is a woman or to a man because he is a man. But the natural capacities are distributed alike among both creatures, and women naturally share in all pursuits and men in all – yet for all the woman is weaker than the man.[15]

The only distinction which Plato wishes to hold on to is that men are stronger than women. From the context, it is not entirely clear what this strength means: it could be solely a matter of physical strength or it could also include mental and emotional strengths.

Plato's view on the nature of men and women can be considered to be quite revolutionary. Hardly any other philosopher before or after him has said that in principle there are no differences in the abilities of men and women and hence no special areas in which they should operate to the exclusion of the other gender. Women can be educated to perform any role and task within the state of which they prove to be capable: of being teachers, musicians, philosophers, rulers, in short, anything.

Plato's next step in the reconsideration of the division of labour between men and women is the reorganisation of the family structure, which, he warns, "...is a far bigger paradox than the other, and provokes more distrust as to its possibility and utility".[16]

This second step is to eliminate monogamous marriage, the traditional family structure, and, ultimately, private possessions. Men and women are to live together not in individual family units, but everyone of the same age is brother and sister to each other. People of different generations are parents and children to each other. Only those of the same generation are to be brought together by the state solely for the purpose of reproduction. The state is to perform a type of genetic engineering when bringing males and females together, ensuring that the best couples will produce the best children and that an unsuitable male or female will not have children with a suitable male or female. These matters are to be arranged discreetly, even if this involves, as Plato says "falsehood and deception".[17] After the children are born, they are to be taken care of by nurses and the children are to call all the children born in their age bracket brothers and sisters, all those capable of being their parents by age, their parents. Private property too is to be abolished, all things being held in common. As a result of the elimination of the traditional family, women would be freed from the task of taking care of their families and homes.

Thus the state provides for the education of women according to their abilities and allows women to fulfill the roles in society for which they have been trained. There are, however, a number of questions which can be asked about Plato's ideas. In the first place, Plato may not be as revolutionary as he appears to be on first sight. An indication of this is the way he writes. The style he uses to speak of men and women is very traditional. The point of view and the standard from out of which is spoken is male. For example, the question is posed "...whether female human nature is capable of sharing with the male all tasks or none at all...", implying that the point of departure as well as the standard lies in male nature and tasks.[18] Plato could be writing in this way because his point of departure is in the prejudices of his society in his time. But is he actually aware of the fact that he is doing this? That it is possible to doubt this is apparent from another example of a traditional style of speaking about men and women, this time with reference to the ideal situation in his city state of the future. Despite the fact that women and men are to perform the same tasks according to their abilities, men are still spoken of as the ones who "have" women. Socrates, for example, states that, "This...is the manner of the community of wives and children among the guardians".[19] But women were supposed to be able to become guardians on an equal basis with men. In addition, even though men and women are to share tasks equally, the text assumes that the people running the communal care centers for children will be women.

A second question which can be raised concerns the practical implications of Plato's views. Plato is confronted with the great task of combining the idea of equal natures, education and roles for men and women with a social structure. Is it desirable to eliminate the realm of the private, of the family? Or, putting it in another way, is it right that the price people must pay to let women have more opportunities is the loss of the private realm? Is the home not a safe haven for people to return to from their participation in the public realm? Is it not the best place to raise children? Is the family not the basic source of wealth and stability in the state? These questions, some of which were also posed by Aristotle in his critique of Plato's *Republic*, have been repeatedly asked of Plato and "communal" theorists up to the present day.

Thirdly, many contemporary women would prefer Plato to have said that men must change *their* roles by doing their share in the private realm as a way to free women for other tasks. In our society, the practical solution for the division of labour when women work outside the home has been sought in this direction. But this solution also has its drawbacks. Is combining tasks within and outside the home possible or does it mean a greater workload and stress all around? Are the domestic tasks shared fairly between men and women? A great deal of research in the last few years shows that this is not the case. Women in fact end up doing both the work in the home and work outside the home. Either the consciousness of men must be raised to a higher level on this point or a more sophisticated solution must be found.[20]

Perhaps raising these questions elicits the thought that it is *very* hard to know "what women want", to quote Freud. Today, feminist perspectives on the role of women focus on maintaining both the private and the public sphere. But both theoretically and practically it is hard to function in both. Men tend to leave the practical problems of running the household and raising the children to women and women tend to do most of the work. Plato was at least on the right track when he said that the issue of equal opportunities and roles for all people, male and female, is something both genders must think about and work on together.

6 Incidental References to Women in Plato's Work

Despite the his radical view of women in the *Republic*, feminist theorists are not totally convinced that Plato's philosophy as a whole presents a positive image of women. In the earlier sections of this chapter, I have already pointed out that there is sometimes ambiguity in Plato's comments on women. There are also several incidental references to women in Plato's work which are ironic and not very flattering. It is however important to note that these are passing remarks made by all sorts of characters in the dialogues, so they may not necessarily reflect Plato's views. They do seem to be able to be fitted into a pattern: when women are criticised it is mostly in terms of their lesser capacity for reasoning.[21]

The idea that women are less rational than men takes on different forms. Women, as in the passage in the *Phaedo* discussed above, are seen as less in control of their emotions than men. For Plato, controlling emotions is not only a matter of strength of character but also of the power of reason which enables a person to rise above a situation. Emotions are seen as direct responses to a situation, while using reason results in an indirect or delayed response, which, for Plato, is of greater value.

Another way in which women are seen as less rational is when certain ideas are attributed to women, implying that women have no real knowledge of things, but that they tend to use lower forms of reason, such as speaking in clichés or forming opinions which are not rationally based. An example of this is the remark in *Letters VIII* where it is stated that: "The usage that applies the term "happy" to the rich is itself miserable, being a foolish usage of women and children, and it renders miserable those that put confidence in it".[22] On the other hand, to Plato's credit, he sometimes praises the insight of women such as in the following passage in the Gorgias: "Perhaps the true man should ignore this question of living for a certain span of years and should not be so enamoured of life, but should leave these things to God and, trusting the womenfolk who say that no man whatever could escape his destiny, should consider the ensuing question..."[23]

Finally, women are sometimes seen as less honourable, courageous or decent than men. This characteristic can perhaps also be linked to their lesser power of reason because rationality is the basis for a strong character. An example of this is the passage in the *Republic* in which instructions are given for the education of the male guardians. Since people who imitate others may perhaps end up taking on the characteristics of those whom they imitate, the guardians should, "...from childhood up imitate what is appropriate to them – men, that is, who are brave, sober, pious, free, and all things of that kind...". They are not, "...being men, to play the parts of women and imitate a woman young or old wrangling with her husband, defying heaven, loudly boasting, fortunate in her own conceit, or involved in misfortune and possessed by grief and lamentation – still less a woman that is sick, in love, or in labor".[24] Perhaps this comment says more about the stock characters of Greek theatre than about Plato's own view of women, but nevertheless, Plato is saying that men should imitate the qualities of good men. Women are not seen as suitable for imitation, that is, in a deeper sense, they are not seen as suitable role models for worthy men.

On the other hand, Plato mentions some women who do not have weaker characters than men. An example of this is Alcestis who sacrificed her life for her husband. Both the gods and mankind were impressed by her courage: "But hers was accounted so great a sacrifice, not only by mankind but by the gods, that in recognition of her magnanimity it was granted – and among the many doers of noble deeds there is only the merest handful to whom such grace is given – that her soul should rise again from the Stygian depths."[25] It may be relevant to note that the courage of Alcestis is told of in the context of a story about the courage which people receive from the power of love: perhaps an area in which women have extra strength.

Plato also thinks that in a metaphysical sense women are of less value than men. He relates in the *Timaeus* that in the process of reincarnation, souls return to female bodies if they were not good enough to be reincarnated as men: "He who lived well during his appointed time was to return and dwell in his native star, and there he would have a blessed and congenial existence. But if he failed in attaining this, at the second birth he would pass into a woman, and if, when in that state of being, he did not desist from evil, he would continually be changed into some brute who resembled him in the evil nature which he had acquired..."[26] That this doctrine is to be taken seriously is indicated by the fact that it is repeated another two times in the course of the dialogue.

From this small selection from the incidental references to women in Plato's dialogues, I think it must be concluded that in all fairness we have a hung jury. Some references are flattering, others are ambiguous, some others are not positive. Plato also makes distinctions among men, as we have seen, describing them in both flattering and non-flattering ways. Perhaps it is more important to note that the references to women are very much fewer than those to men, indicating that Plato was writing mainly about men and for men.

7   Theoretical Contexts for a Feminist Interpretation of Plato

Attempts have been made in the literature to account for Plato's seemingly contradictory statements about women by creating a theoretical context in which to read them. A number of these theories focus on Plato's preference for a male world with male values.

One can consider Plato's view of women in the context of the way in which he sees people and values in general. As the passage in the *Symposium*, discussed above, indicates, Plato believes that human beings, living between heaven and earth, should orient themselves to the higher spheres. This implies a hierarchical view of people in which people with a higher and more rational orientation are better than those without one. Leaving the earthly behind, the best people should orient themselves to contemplating the Good, the Beautiful and the True.

Such a view of people means that women will generally speaking be considered to have less value than men. According to Plato, one is oriented to the higher realms primarily through a theoretical and preferably philosophical education, an education almost exclusively available to men in ancient Greece. Despite the beautiful words in the *Republic* in which Plato emphasises the equal talents of men and women, even citing the example of "lover of wisdom" as being within feminine reach, the fact of the matter was that women were excluded from participation in Socrates' dialogues and from attending Plato's Academy. Proof of this is the story of Axiothea. Inspired by reading of the equality of man and woman in Plato's *Republic*, Axiothea, according to Themistius, travelled from Arcadia to Athens to study with Plato. Dichaearchus relates that she had to dress as a man to be admitted to Plato's lectures. Her dressing as a man was not a personal eccentricity but this fact was used in ancient times by Dichaearchus to show the discrepancy between Plato's theories and practice.[27]

Not only are women excluded from those realms which, in Plato's view, would give them equal status to men, they are also, as we saw, identified with the spheres which are considered to be lower: the realm of the everyday world and of the natural realm of reproduction. The question here, however, is, why these realms are seen as "lower".

In the history of philosophy, many philosophers have criticised Plato on the point of his otherwordly view of people and reality and the resulting value system. In this sense, the feminist critique of Plato forms part of an older philosophical discussion. All those who would like a greater appreciation for the concrete, the earthly, the everyday world, accuse Plato of too great an emphasis on the non-physical, the non-empirical, the abstract. I think that there are two sides to such a philosophical critique, a positive and a negative one. On the positive side, I think that the tendency of contemporary philosophy to renounce high levels of abstraction, too much otherwordliness in philosophical thought, and the devaluation of everyday life and physical reality, is positive because this gives more value to the concrete and specific sides of philosophical thought. On the negative side, the contemporary philosophical orientation to the earthly, everyday reality and the non-rational or irrational sides of life can also be considered to be a luxury which we can now afford, but which was not a luxury in Plato's time. By this I mean that in contemporary culture there is more academic, scientific and abstract activity going on than ever before in the history of humankind. For Plato and his time, abstract knowledge, truth, and mental values were not as developed and were vitally needed in order to further knowledge of people, society, and the world. We can see how important Plato considers education and rationality in his story of the allegory of the cave. Here he argues that it is the task of the philosopher to lead people away from their fascination with the concrete, earthly world of mere appearances to the realm of insight and truth. In the allegory of the cave, Plato argues that it is the task of the intellectual to see things the way they really are. I think that in our time we sometimes take the immense intellectual achievements on which our culture is built for granted. We should therefore not look down on the ideals which Plato formulates for the development of philosophical, theoretical and scientific thought. After all, there is still more we do not know than we know and as to the high regard which Plato had for ethics, we could also learn something. Nevertheless, from out of our position of relative luxury with regard to the achievements of abstract rationality, we now have the freedom to say that there is more in the world than that which Plato's philosophy was directed to. Reason is more than abstraction and separation from the everyday world.

L. Irigaray has written a psychoanalysis of Plato's allegory of the cave. She regards this allegory as the symbolical expression of the male desire to distance himself from the womb, the earthly, and the feminine. By associating himself with the otherworldly, abstract, spiritual, presumably higher, masculine realm, he seeks to find and affirm his male identity.[28] If Irigaray's psychoanalytical categories can be accepted, it means that Plato does separate the feminine from the masculine realms of reason and knowledge. His mistake is perhaps in thinking that a positive appreciation of knowledge and abstraction implies excluding women. It is of course possible to have a positive appreciation of both men and women, abstract and concrete, and to realise that it is not necessary to associate one gender with a certain type of thought or approach to reality.

Notes

1 M. Pellikaan-Engel, "Socrates' Blind Spots", in: M. Pellikaan-Engel, ed. *Against Patriarchal Thinking*. Amsterdam, VU University Press, 1992, p. 5-11. This is a revised and shortened version of the original Dutch article, "De verhouding Socrates-Xanthippe in filosofisch perspectief", *Feminisme Filosofie*, Leusden, The Netherlands, Internationale School voor Wijsbegeerte, 1979, p. 7-28.

2 Plato, *Collected Dialogues*, transl. by Hamilton and Cairns. Princeton, Princeton University Press, 1973, p. 43. *Phaedo* 60a-b.

3 F. Nietzsche, *Zur Genealogie der Moral*, in: *Nietzsches Werke*. ed. by Gerhard Stenzel. Salzburg, Bergland, volume 2, p. 869-870. (Third Essay, paragraph 7).

4 G. Ménage, *The History of Women Philosophers. (Historia Mulierum Philosopharum)*. transl. by B.H. Zedler. Lanham/London, University Press of America, 1984. p. 6-8.

5 Plato, *Collected Dialogues*. transl. by Hamilton and Cairns. Princeton, Princeton University Press, 1973, p. 187-189 and p. 198-199. *Menexenus* 235e-238a, 249d-e.

6 For a discussion concerning the historical existence of Diotima, see M.E. Waithe, *A History of Women Philosophers. Vol. I*, 600 B.C. – 500 AD. Dordrecht/Lancaster/London, Martinus Nijhoff, 1987, p. 91-114. Gilles Ménage also mentions Diotima and gives

further ancient references to her. See: *The History of Women Philosophers.* transl. by Beatrice H. Zedler, Lanham/London, Univesity Press of America, 1984, p. 9 and 100.

7 Plato, *Collected Dialogues,* transl. by Hamilton and Cairns. Princeton, Princeton University Press, 1973, p. 553-563. *Symposium* 201d-212b.

8 The "weakness" of association when it involves the female is also demonstrated in the *Symposium* in the story of Aristophanes concerning love. The famous story relates that the power of human beings makes the gods jealous. As a result, the gods decide to cut human beings in half: some are cut as male-male, some as male-female, others as female-female. Love is the desire to be reunited with one's other half. Aristophanes notes that the female-female link is the weakest of the combinations, with the male-male as the strongest. See: Plato, *Collected Dialogues,* transl. by Hamilton and Cairns. Princeton, Princeton University Press, 1973, p. 542-546. *Symposium* 189c-193d.

9 L. Irigaray, *Speculum. Of the Other Woman.* transl. by Gillian C. Gill. Ithaca, Cornell University Press, 1985, p. 133-146. See also the third part of this book, "Plato's Hystera", p. 243-364.

10 D. Wender, in her article, "Plato: Misogynist, Paedophile, and Feminist", *Arethusa* 6 (1973), p. 82, does not discuss the *Symposium*, because she says, "...it seems to me doubtful that any speaker in that dialogue (including Socrates-Diotima but perhaps excluding Alcibiades) wholly represents Plato's view."

11 For a feminist interpretation of the *Republic,* see: J.B. Elshtain, *Public Man, Private Woman: Women in Social and Political Thought.* Princeton, Princeton University Press, 1981, p. 19-41.

12 Plato, *Collected Dialogues.* transl. by Hamilton and Cairns. Princeton, Princeton University Press, 1973, p. 695. *Republic* v, 456b-c.

13 Plato, *Collected Dialogues.* transl. by Hamilton and Cairns. Princeton, Princeton University Press, 1973, p. 694. *Republic* v 455a.

14 Plato, *Collected Dialogues.* transl. by Hamiton and Cairns. Princeton, Princeton University Press, 1973, p. 694. *Republic* v 455b-e.

15 Plato, *Collected Dialogues.* transl. by Hamilton and Cairns. Princeton, Princeton University Press, 1973, p. 694. *Republic* v 455d-e.

16 Plato, *Collected Dialogues.* transl. by Hamilton and Cairns. Princeton, Princeton University Press, 1973, p. 696-697. *Republic* v 457d.

17 Plato, *Collected Dialogues.* transl. by Hamilton and Cairns. Princeton, Princeton University Press, 1973, p. 698. *Republic* v 459c-d. The use of "falsehood and deception" by a philosopher oriented to the Idea of the Good has troubled some commentators. See for example Roger Trigg, *Ideas of Human Nature.* Oxford, Blackwell, p. 18. Trigg speaks here of the "surprising ruthlessness" of Socrates.

18 Plato, *Collected Dialogues*. transl. by Hamilton and Cairns. Princeton, Princeton University Press, 1973, p. 691, 692. *Republic* v, 451e-452a and 453a.

19 Plato, *Collected Dialogues*. transl. by Hamilton and Cairns. Princeton, Princeton University Press, 1973, p. 701. *Republic* v 461e.

20 Arlie Hochschild, *The Second Shift*. Viking, 1989.

21 For a number of references to women in Plato's dialogues, see: Apology 35a-b; Cratylus 414a, 418b, 430b-431c; Critias 110a-c, 112d; Epistle VII 349d, Epistle VIII 355c; Gorgias 502d, 512d-e; Hippias, Greater, 286a, Laws I 637b-e, Laws II 658a-d, 669c, Laws III 680b-e, 694d-695b, Laws v 731d, 739c, Laws VI 774a-776b, 780e, 781a-785b, Laws VII 788a-797, 802e, 804e, 805a-d, 806a-b, 813e, 814b, Laws VIII 803c, 804c-806c, 806d-808c, 808d-809a, 828c, 829b-e, 833c-e, Laws XI 930a, 932b, Laws XII 944d-e.; Lysis 208d; Menexenus 235e-238a, 249d-e; Meno 71e-73b, 99d; Phaedo 60a-b, 116b, 117d-e; Protagoras 342d; Republic I 329b-c; Republic II 360a-b; Republic III 387e-388a, 395d-e, 398e; Republic IV 431b-c; Republic v 449c, 451b-c, 451d-e, 451e-452a, 453, 454d-e, 455b-e, 456b, 457a-b, 457c-d, 458c-e, 459d-e, 460c, 461e, 464b, 466c-e, 471d; Republic VII 540c; Republic VIII 548a-b, 549c-d, 563b-d, 605d-e; Theatetus 176b; Symposium 179b-e, 176e, 180d-181e, 189c-193d; Timaeus 18c, 42b-c, 76d-e, 90e-91a.

22 Plato, *Collected Dialogues*. transl. by Hamilton and Cairns. Princeton, Princeton University Press, 1973, p. 1601. *Epistle* VIII 355c.

23 Plato, *Collected Dialogues*. transl. by Hamilton and Cairns. Princeton, Princeton University Press, 1973, p. 294. *Gorgias* 355e.

24 Plato, *Collected Dialogues*. transl. by Hamilton and Cairns. Princeton, Princeton University Press, 1973, p. 640. *Republic* III 395c-e.

25 Plato, *Collected Dialogues*. transl. by Hamilton and Cairns. Princeton, Princeton University Press, 1973, p. 533. *Symposium* 179b-c.

26 Plato, *Collected Dialogues*. transl. by Hamilton and Cairns. Princeton, Princeton University Press, 1973, p. 1171. *Timaeus* 42b-c. See also *Timaeus* 76d-e (p. 1198) and 90e-91a (p. 1209-1210).

27 M.E. Waithe, *A History of Women Philosophers. Vol.* 1, 600 B.C. – 500 AD. Dordrecht, Lancaster, London, Martinus Nijhoff, 1987, p. 205-206.

28 L. Irigaray, *Speculum. Of the Other Woman*. transl. by Gillian C. Gill. Ithaca, Cornell University Press, 1985, p. 243-364. For a more detailed discussion of Plato's allegory of the cave and possible interpretations of this story, see chapter 9.

3 Aristotle. The Nature of Woman and her Role in Society

1 Introduction

As we saw in the previous chapter, Plato argues that his view of women in the *Republic* is based on a general view of human nature. Aristotle (384-322 B.C.) too believes that it is necessary to create a philosophy of society based on the nature of people, that is, on the composition of their souls. Like Plato, he attempts to justify giving people roles in society which reflect their tendencies and capacities for fulfilling these roles. In this sense, he wishes to create a rational ground for a philosophy of society. With respect to women, such an approach leads Aristotle to ask and answer the same kind of questions as Plato: "Do women and men differ in their natures?" "Would such a difference lead to them fulfilling different roles in society?" Aristotle has, however, a very different concept of feminine nature than Plato. Aristotle is of importance in the history of views on women because he created an influential approach which assigned women a traditional role.

In this chapter, I will begin by presenting Aristotle's critique of Plato's *Republic* in his book, the *Politics*. In the second half of this chapter, anticipating another debate, I will describe Aristotle's view of women as presented in *On the Generation of Animals*, his biology. Aristotle's biological theories concerning women will be taken up again in the next chapter in which I will discuss the use made of them by the medieval theologian and philosopher, St. Thomas Aquinas.

2 Aristotle's Critique of Plato

In his *Politics*, Aristotle begins with a discussion on the nature of the state. He believes that the basis of the state is the traditional family structure, with the woman in the home, responsible for the household management and the care of the young children. The task of the man is to obtain and maintain property and wealth, which is held by the family and forms the basis of wealth in society.[1]

Fundamental to the family, as well as to the state, is ruling: "For that some should rule and others be ruled is a thing not only necessary, but expedient; from the hour of their birth, some are marked out for subjection, others for rule".[2] Aristotle considers various sorts of ruling relationships: of a better workman over another workman, of the soul over the body, of men over animals. He then says: "Again, the male is by nature superior, and the female inferior; and the one rules, and the other is ruled; this principle, of necessity, extends to all mankind".[3] The argument here is "from nature". Aristotle illustrates his concept of ruling with reference to the category of masters and slaves, saying that, "It is clear, then, that some men are by nature free, and others slaves, and that for these latter slavery is both expedient and right".[4] He does, however, modify his position quickly, saying that at times slavery may be just the bad luck of being captured in war, but nevertheless, this was most likely a just fate because the slave has no reasoning capacity for himself, hence his slavery and need to be ruled. The ruling relationship is based on the power of reason in the rulers and the ruled. Because the slave lacks his own power of reason, the rule over slaves is despotical or tyrannical. A slave simply needs to be told what to do and is to do what he or she is told.

In the *Politics*, Aristotle calls the rule of a man over his wife constitutional because in this form of ruling there is an element of equality and the possession of certain rights. Men and women are to some extent equal and women have some capacity for reason, but women have less power of reason than men. While in men reason often prevails over irrationality, in women, irrationality is stronger.[5] A man is, therefore, superior to his wife and rules over her in the same way as in a constitutional state some citizens rule over other citizens. In this sense, men and women are, according to Aristotle, always unequal. Nevertheless, a characteristic of constitutional rule is that although the better rule over others, the ruled still have something to say about the governing process. In the *Nichomachean Ethics*, Aristotle also discusses the nature of the rule of the husband over the wife and here he calls this type of rule aristocratic. The reason he gives for this is that "...the man rules in accordance with his worth, and in those matters in which a man should rule, but the matters that befit a woman he hands over to her." It is possible that in marriage other forms of governing replace aristocratic rule. When a man rules over everything, the rule in the marriage is that of oligarchy. Sometimes the woman rules because she is an heiress and that too is oligarchic rule. Aristotle defines oligarchy as ruling "...not in virtue of excellence but due to wealth and power..."[6]

The rule of a father over his children is royal.[7] Children are not yet fully in possession of their reasoning capacities; the rule is, however, not despotical, because, unlike in the case of slaves, children are in principle capable of developing their reason. The father's rule is not constitutional either because a child's reason is not yet developed fully enough to participate democratically in the decision making process.

In the *Nichomachean Ethics*, Aristotle does not restrict himself to describing the formal relationships in the family in terms of rule but he also introduces the notion of friendship. Friendship relationships are described by him in the same way as he describes the relationships among people in the household, that is, in terms of a hierarchy. There are two forms of friendship, according to Aristotle, that of equality between the friends, the ideal form, and that of relative inequality. The relationships in the family are friendships of inequality, of father to son, elder and younger, man to wife and, as he states, "of ruler to subject". These different forms of relationships differ according to the nature of the inequality and the type of relationship between the parties. The relationships between parents and children, father and son, husband and wife all differ in their virtues, their functions, and the type of love between the parties. The members of the family differ in their obliga-tions to each other. For example, children should be grateful to their parents for bringing them into the world. Aristotle then goes on to claim that in these friendships, the loving relationship is also hierarchically coloured: "In all friendships implying inequality the love should also be proportional, i.e., the better should be more loved than he loves, and so should the more useful, and similarly in each of the other cases; for when the love is in proportion to the merit of the parties, then in a sense arises equality, which is certainly held to be characteristic of friendship".[8] Hence, even though friendship in the family is unequal, the true nature of friendship, equality, can be attained when, for example, the better is more loved than the inferior. Aristotle later on repeats his view that there is a hierarchical power relationship in love. He states, "Most people seem, owing to ambition, to wish to be loved rather than to love..."[9]

In the *Politics*, Aristotle argues that the main reason for the organi-sation of a household is virtue and excellence: while the gaining of wealth and property are of importance, these are secondary to forming the character of especially the free persons in the household. He considers the question of whether or not women and children have virtues at all, but decides that they have their own types of virtue which must be formed within the context of the family.[10]

In considering the question of the virtues of women, Aristotle's views differ from those of Socrates. Aristotle argues that women have a different nature from men and hence different virtues. In saying this, he explicitly attacks Socrates' position as formulated in the *Republic* that men and women are in principle capable of the same things and hence have the capacity for having the same virtues. "Clearly, then", he says, "moral virtue belongs to all of them; but the temperance of a man and of a woman, or the courage and justice of a man and of a woman, are not, as Socrates maintained, the same; the courage of a man is shown in commanding, of a woman in obeying. And this holds of all other virtues..." He goes on to add that silence is a woman's glory, but not a man's.[11]

Aristotle continues his discourse with Socrates in the second book of the *Politics*, in which the question concerning what is to be held in common in the state is discussed. He says: "But should a well-ordered state have all things, so far as may be, in common, or some only and not others? For the citizens might conceivably have wives and children and property in common, as Socrates proposes in the *Republic* of Plato. Which is better, our present condition, or the proposed new order of society?"[12] What follows is an attack on Socrates' position. Aristotle argues that Socrates' view of holding all things in common creates difficulties because it changes the role divisions between men and women in the traditional family structure. Aristotle says:

> If Socrates makes the women common, and retains private property, the men will see to the fields, but who will see to the house? And who will do so if the agricultural class have both their property and their wives in common? Once more: it is absurd to argue, from the analogy of the animals, that men and women should follow the same pursuits, for animals have not to manage a household.[13]

Aristotle does, however, in the end insert the following gallant comment: "The discourses of Socrates are never commonplace; they always exhibit grace and originality and thought; but perfection in everything can hardly be expected".[14]

Finally, in the last two books of the *Politics,* Aristotle gives his views on matters such as marriage, the rules for how women are to comport themselves and on the best way in which to educate children.[15]

Aristotle begins by considering the age at which men and women should marry: they should be so matched that the male and female age of procreation ends at the same time. The man should not be able to beget children when the woman is no longer able to bear them. Aristotle also notes that children should not be born of parents who are too old or too young. This rule implies that the male should be older than the female, since males are of course able to produce children for a longer time than females. Aristotle therefore recommends that women marry at age eighteen, men at age thirty-seven.[16] Furthermore, men are to cease begetting children at fifty four or five, since male intelligence, according to Aristotle, begins to decline after age fifty.[17]

He next considers the best time for marriage (winter) and the best type of physical and mental attributes for the male as husband and father. Women who are pregnant should have regular exercise and a proper diet. Aristotle makes the recommendation that: "The first of these prescriptions the legislator will easily carry into effect by requiring that they shall take a walk daily to some temple, where they can worship the gods who preside over birth. Their minds, however, unlike their bodies, they ought to keep quiet, for the offspring derive their natures from their mothers as plants do from the earth".[18]

Aristotle recommends the killing of deformed children and limiting population growth by exposing the children, but, since this is usually forbidden by states, abortion is preferable. He then discusses at length the rearing of children. Aristotle's concerns resemble some of the ones expressed by the Pythagorean school: how to ensure strong children by caring for them soberly and hardening them to life. He suggests, for example, making them bear cold conditions and exposing them only to proper activities and amusements. Children are to do no work or have formal learning until age five and must live at home until age seven. They are to be educated in two phases: from age seven to puberty, from puberty to age twenty-one. Children are to be raised in the home by the mother, but boys are to be educated later in the male world.[19] Aristotle's views on these matters, not surpisingly, are very traditional. Women are to stay in the home and be virtuous like the Pythagorean women.

3   Patterns in Aristotle's View of the Family in the State

It has been noted by critics, feminist and others, that Aristotle's theory of the state and the nature and roles of people within the state tends to justify the customs of his time, in contrast with the views of Plato, which can be considered to be more innovative. Aristotle tends to define the natures of people in terms of the existing social order, a temptation one finds most strongly in the discussion on slavery. The difficulty is that the aim at the outset, to base the filling in of social roles on the concept of nature, becomes circular: the ideas of nature and social role come to be defined in terms of each other. There is then no longer, as Aristotle claimed, an independent "natural" justification for an existing social order.

Aristotle could object to this argument by saying that he believes that the social order of his time is truly the reflection of human nature itself. This implies that the ideal has more or less already been realised and that nothing remains to be thought about concerning nature and culture. This can be an acceptable philosophical position to take, albeit a very conservative one. What is not acceptable is trying to use this as an argument attempting to *prove* this relationship.

These ideas concerning the relationship between nature and culture bring us to the second aspect which we will look at in Aristotle's view of women, the biological. Perhaps the biological account given by Aristotle of women will be able to arrive at a separate definition of male and female nature. As we shall see, however, this is not the case. This is because Aristotle's biology is not an empirical science in the modern sense of the word. Although he does use examples, observations, and empirical data, the method of analysing them is based on a system derived from other parts of his philosophy.

4 Aristotle's Biology of Woman

Aristotle wrote a book on the biology of reproduction, called *On the Generation of Animals*. Although this book is today less well known than Aristotle's works on metaphysics, logic and ethics, its historical impact was considerable, as we shall see in the next chapter in which St. Thomas Aquinas' use of ideas from this book is discussed. Many of Aristotle's ideas can still be found in contemporary thought, primarily because of their lasting influence on Christian theology.

Aristotle opens his discussion of the nature of women by looking at the reasons for the existence of men and women in the first place. The main reason for the human race to be differentiated into two genders is reproduction, as he states at the beginning of Book II of *On the Generation of Animals*.[20]

In speaking of the "first principle of generation", the male and female, Aristotle introduces a number of terms which he identifies with one or the other gender. On the male side, he speaks in terms of "first efficient or moving cause" to which belong "definition and form", better and more divine in its nature, a "superior principle". On the female side, he speaks of "material" on which the male principle "works", an "inferior principle". These terms indicate that Aristotle sees the relative value of male and female as basic to his biological theory of reproduction. This valuation of male and female can be seen as a presupposition of his theory, but, according to Aristotle, it can be concluded from empirical data.

For Aristotle, conception takes place when the male introduces the sperm, the form, in the female. He believes that the female contributes matter for the gestation of the sperm. This matter is menstrual blood which becomes the material support and feeding ground for the unborn child. Later, it is the woman's body which provides the protection and food for the unborn child. Behind these ideas is the image of a plant growing in the soil. The father therefore introduces life, soul, "definition and form" as the first active, superior principle. The mother is the material receptacle of the sperm and hence is a receptive, passive, secondary cause of reproduction.

The reason why the child can be born either male or female is explained by Aristotle by means of differences in the heat of the sperm of the father. Aristotle believes that the hotter a man is, the hotter and hence better, more active and effective, his sperm. The heat of the sperm depends on the good health of the father and even on climactic conditions: a cold wind blowing, for example, cools the sperm. The healthier the father, the warmer the weather at the time of conception, the greater the chance is that the child will be male. A female is born when these ideal conditions are not present. She is, in Aristotle's terminology, a "misbegotten male", in fact, a mistake of nature. As St. Thomas Aquinas in his commentary on this idea of Aristotle makes clear, the reason for seeing the female as "misbegotten" lies in the fact that ideally nature always reproduces "the same".[21] When an offspring has characteristics that deviate from the norm, it is defective. Since the father's sperm is what actually produces the child, the child should ideally resemble the father, and hence should always be male. This "mistake" of nature, however, is necessary because women are needed for reproduction.

The superiority of males to females, according to Aristotle, is also evident from differences in their development. Female children seem to be stronger and develop more quickly than males. But Aristotle notes that the inferior and cold, the female, only demonstrates its inferiority by its faster development. The male develops more slowly but surely than the female.[22]

5   Matter and Form, Metaphysics, Politics and Biology

It has been extensively, and I think successfully, argued that the prejudices present in Aristotle's biology are supported by his metaphysics.[23] To demonstrate this, critics have concentrated on Aristotle's notion of matter and form. Aristotle is often praised for the fact that he did not see matter and form as totally separate entities, as did Plato, and that as a result he does not have such an abstract and otherwordly philosophy as Plato. In light of the discussion held in the previous chapter concerning the relationship in Plato's philosophy between abstraction and otherwordliness and a view of women as lesser than men, Aristotle's philosophy would seem to offer women a better deal.[24] But this is not entirely true. Aristotle does distinguish between matter and form and this distinction is fundamental to his view of women. Matter and form, more "empirical" in Aristotle, are intertwined, yet distinguishable components of all things.

In the matter-form model of metaphysics, the matter is the "material" component of an object. Form is the shape of the object. All extended things have matter, but that which makes the matter of, say a chair, different from that of a table is that they have different forms. Form makes a thing a specific entity and thus allows us to be able to say what a thing is. The form of an object is therefore also that which makes it knowable. Taking this one step further, Aristotle identifies the concept of form with knowledge, mind, and spirit itself.

Applying these metaphysical ideas to the texts under consideration, Aristotle notes that the woman is the material cause of generation. She thus represents the lower principle, matter, and the male represents the higher principle, form. Hence the notions of inferiority and superiority, passivity and activity, material basis and the identification of the male with life and spirit. From this primary distinction, many of the other features of Aristotle's analysis of male and female can be understood: the idea that the male is hot, the female cold, the male perfectly formed, the female defective.

If one accepts the argument that there is a link between Aristotle's metaphysics and his biology, then this means that Aristotle's philosophy is a whole which holds together the analyses of reality (metaphysics), society (as in the passages from the *Politics* discussed earlier) and biology (as in the passages from *De Generatione Animalium* which were mentioned) in one conceptual framework. This means that, just as in Plato, hierarchical structures are present in all three of these areas in Aristotle's thought.

Another aspect of the wider philosophical picture is the role which reason plays in relation to nature. In the *Politics*, as we saw, males are to govern since they by nature have the greatest amount of reason. Also with respect to biology, reason is important because the ordering of nature is rational in the sense that it accords with certain principles of purpose. There is, in other words, a rationality in man, society and nature, a rationality which the philosopher can discover.

Part of this notion of rationality is the concept of *telos*, end or goal. All things move towards the goal of their proper actualisation. From the analyses which Aristotle gives of female nature, it is clear that her nature has specific forms of self-realisation: in society, to function within the family structure, in biology, to reproduce. Women, as critics have pointed out, are in no position in Aristotle's system to determine for themselves what they would like to be and do. That would be unnatural, create a kind of anarchy, since all things and people must order themselves or be ordered according to their own nature and Aristotle sees himself as giving the right description of that nature. In this sense, contrary to Plato's views on these matters, as presented in the *Republic*, women do not have a great deal of freedom for self-realisation in Aristotle's world.[25]

Rightly or wrongly, Aristotle has gone into history as rather notori-ous when it comes to his views on women. Critics including men, have, throughout the centuries, commented on his sexism. But there has also been a considerable amount of historical speculation about, and, inter-estingly, many famous depictions on tapestries, paintings and engrav-ings of, his private life with Phyllis.[26] Aristotle had a relationship with Phyllis which, if the gossip is true, does not exactly mirror his macho views. But the most significant fact about Aristotle's views on women, as we shall see in the next chapter, is their disproportionate influence on western thought.

Notes

1   Aristotle, *Politica. The Works of Aristotle*. ed. by W.D. Ross. Oxford, Clarendon Press, 1952. Vol. 10. Book I, 4, 1253b, 22.

2   Aristotle, *Politica. The Works of Aristotle*. ed. by W.D. Ross. Oxford, Clarendon Press, 1952. Vol. 10. Book I, 5, 1254a, 21-24.

3   Aristotle, *Politica. The Works of Aristotle*. ed. by W.D. Ross. Oxford, Clarendon Press, 1952. Vol. 10. Book I, 5, 1254b, 12-16.

4   Aristotle, *Politica. The Works of Aristotle*. ed. by W.D. Ross. Oxford, Clarendon Press, 1952. Vol. 10. Book I, 5, 1255a, 1-3. See also: W.W. Fortenbaugh, "Aristotle on Slaves and Women", in J. Barnes, et. al., eds., *Articles on Aristotle. Vol. 2: Ethics and Politics*. London, Duckworth, 1977, p. 135-139.

5   It is, however, important to note that, according to Aristotle, all humans, with the possible exception of slaves, have a rational part to their soul. In *De Anima*, Aristotle describes the human soul as having a tripartite structure, with a vegetative, sensitive and rational component.

6 Aristotle, *Ethica Nicomachea. The Works of Aristotle.* ed. by W.D. Ross. Oxford, Clarendon Press, 1954, Vol. 9. Book VIII, 10, 1160b 33-40 to 1161a 1-3.

7 Aristotle, *Politica. The Works of Aristotle.* ed. by W.D. Ross. Oxford, Clarendon Press, 1952. Vol. 10. Book I, 12, 1259a-1259b, 37-40 and 1-17.

8 Aristotle, *Ethica Nichomachea. The Works of Aristotle.* ed. by W.D. Ross. Oxford, Clarendon Press, 1954. Vol. 9. Book VIII, 7, 1158b 12-29.

9 Aristotle, *Ethica Nichomachea. The Works of Aristotle.* ed. by W.D. Ross. Oxford, Clarendon Press, 1954. Vol. 9. Book VIII, 8, 1159a 14-15.

10 Aristotle, *Politica. The Works of Aristotle.* ed. by W.D. Ross. Oxford, Clarendon Press, 1952. Vol. 10. Book I, 13, 1259b-1260a-b.

11 Aristotle, *Politica. The Works of Aristotle.* ed. by W.D. Ross. Oxford, Clarendon Press, 1952. Vol. 10. Book I, 1260a

12 Aristotle, *Politica. The Works of Aristotle.* ed. by W.D. Ross. Oxford, Clarendon Press, 1952. Vol. 10. Book II, 1, 1261a, 3-7.

13 Aristotle, *Politica. The Works of Aristotle.* ed. by W.D. Ross. Oxford, Clarendon Press, 1952. Vol. 10. Book II, 5, 1264b, 1-7.

14 Aristotle, *Politica. The Works of Aristotle.* ed. by W.D. Ross. Oxford, Clarendon Press, 1952. Vol. 10. Book II, 5, 1265a, 10-12.

15 Aristotle, *Politica. The Works of Aristotle.* ed. by W.D. Ross. Oxford, Clarendon Press, 1952. Vol. 10. Books VII and VIII.

16 Aristotle, *Politica. The Works of Aristotle.* ed. by W.D. Ross. Oxford, Clarendon Press, 1952. Vol. 10. Book VII, 16, 1334b 28-1335a 40. According to Horowitz, the usual age of marriage for men in Athens at the time of Aristotle was 30, for women 14-16. M.C. Horowitz, "Aristotle and Woman", *Journal of the History of Biology* 9 (1976, 2), p. 198, footnote 47.

17 Aristotle, *Politica. The Works of Aristotle.* ed. by W.D. Ross. Oxford, Clarendon Press, 1952. Vol. 10. Book VII 16, 1335b 32-36.

18 Aristotle, *Politica. The Works of Aristotle.* ed. by W.d. Ross. Oxford, Clarendon Press, 1952. Vol. 10. Book VII, 16, 1335b 14-19. The Ross edition has a footnote to this passage, referring to Plato's *Laws*, VII, 789e. In 789d the Athenian asks, "Would you have us raise a laugh by express statutes directing the pregnant mother to take constitutionals...?" The text continues with an interesting discussion on mothers, nurses and infant behaviour.

19 Aristotle, *Politica. The Works of Aristotle.* ed. by W.D. Ross. Oxford, Clarendon Press, 1952. Vol. 10. Book VIII.

20 Aristotle, *De Generatione Animalium. The Works of Aristotle.* ed. by W.D. Ross. Oxford, Clarendon Press, 1949. Vol. 5. Book II.

21 St. Thomas Aquinas, *Summa Theologica,* Question 92, article 1. transl. by the Fathers of the English Dominican Province. London, Burns, Oates and Washbourne, 1911. Vol. 4, p. 275-276. Here St. Thomas Aquinas states, "As regards the individual nature, woman is defective and misbegotten, for the active force in the male seed tends to the production of a perfect likeness in the masculine sex; while the production of woman comes from defect in the active force or from some material indisposition, or even from some external influence; such that of a south wind, which is moist, as the Philosopher observes". (*De. Gener. Animal.* iv. 2).

22 Aristotle, *De Generatione Animalium. The Works of Aristotle.* ed. by W.D. Ross. Oxford, Clarendon Press, 1949. Vol. 5. Book II, 775a, 5-23.

23 See for example, Horowitz, M.C. "Aristotle and Woman", *Journal of the History of Biology* 9 (1976, 2), p. 183-213. Lange, L. "Woman is not a Rational Animal: On Aristotle's Biology of Reproduction", in: S. Harding and M. Hintikka, eds., *Discovering Reality.* Dordrecht, Reidel, 1983. p. 1-15. Matthews, G.B. "Gender and Essence in Aristotle", *Australasian Journal of Philosophy,* Supplement to vol. 64, June 1986. p. 16-25. Spelman, E. "Aristotle and the Politicization of the Soul", in: S. Harding and M. Hintikka, eds., *Discovering Reality.* Dordrecht, Reidel, 1983. p. 17-30. M.A. Warren, "Aristotle", *The Nature of Woman.* California, Edgepress, 1980, p. 34-39.

24 G. Lloyd, *The Man of Reason. "Male" and "Female" in Western Philosophy.* London, Methuen, 1984, p. 7-9.

25 L. Irigaray, *Speculum. Of the Other Woman.* transl. by Gillian C. Gill. Ithaca, New York, Cornell University Press, 1985, p. 160-167.

26 For example, the tapestry of Freiburg and the well-known engraving of Aristotle and Phyllis by A. Dürer. The engraving of Phyllis riding Aristotle by Dürer is reproduced on the cover of G. Lloyd, *The Man of Reason. "Male" and "Female" in Western Philosophy.* London, Methuen, 1984. In the article by Maryanne Cline Horowitz, "Aristotle and Woman", *Journal of the History of Biology* 9, (1976, 2), p. 183-213, an engraving of the same theme by the Renaissance artist Martin Zatzinger can be found on p. 190.

4 St. Thomas Aquinas. The Theology of Woman

1 Introduction

In the Middle Ages, as in no other period in the history of western philosophy, philosophy and theology go hand in hand. The questions concerning the nature of women and their role in society in this time are concentrated on the interpretation of Bible passages which speak of women.

There are a number of passages in the Bible which mention women. The first chapters of Genesis which describe the creation of woman, the fall into sin and the resulting curse on mankind are important for a theological view of women. As we shall see in this chapter, all sorts of questions were raised as to the significance of these passages for a view of women. Why was Eve created out of Adam's rib and not, like Adam, from out of the earth? What does the Bible mean when it says that Eve was created as a "help meet" for Adam? Why did Eve succumb to the temptation of Satan before Adam did? Does this mean that she was weaker and less rational than Adam? Why would God create, in a perfect creation, a less perfect creature than Adam himself? If Eve was indeed less rational and more open to temptation, does she have a soul in the same sense as Adam? To what extent was she then made in the image of God? What was the relationship like between Adam and Eve: did they experience sexual-sensual pleasure before the fall into sin?[1]

Questions also arose concerning the implications of the fall into sin in terms of the curse that was placed on the woman, man, and the snake after the fall. Women, the Biblical judgment relates, are cursed by the fact that they are to beget children in pain and, because their desire is for their husbands, are to be ruled by them. What is the implication of the latter curse: is this the correct order of things in the world and therefore a justification for the male ruling over the female? It is obvious that the interpretation of this text is of vital importance because it may or may not give men a theological reason for male domination.

Also relevant to a view of women are Old Testament passages which speak of marriage and polygamy. Why was polygamy practised in ancient times and why it is was later forbidden? Other well-known passages are the text at the end of the book of Proverbs describing the ideal wife and the references to women in the Song of Songs. The passages in the New Testament book of Revelation referring to the notion of the Church as the bride of Christ are interpreted as relating back to the stories of a man and his bride in the Song of Songs.

In the New Testament, of interest are the gospel story of Mary and the birth of Christ, Christ's contacts with women and his references to women, and Pauline teachings concerning marriage, the relationship between husband and wife, and the role of women in the Church.

The theology of Mary only began to emerge in the late Middle Ages, but earlier, the main theological issues concerning women involved discussions of the views expressed by St. Paul. What did Paul mean when he said that it was better to remain single than to marry? In no other period of western culture was this advice taken so seriously as in the Middle Ages. What is the role of women in the Church, especially in terms of religious offices and orders? It has been argued that in the course of the Middle Ages one can observe a gradual growth of control of men over women in the Church hierarchy. While in the very early period, women still performed the sacraments, this was later to become an exclusively male task. Female religious orders were usually placed under the supervision of the neighbouring male order.[2]

Besides questions concerning the interpretation of Bible passages, the issue was discussed of the hermeneutic principles to be applied when reading them. The Bible passages mentioned can be read literally or allegorically. The distinction between reading a passage literally or allegorically may sometimes be difficult to draw.[3] The choice of the way in which these passages are to be treated hermeneutically has, however, implications for the view of women. This is because at least some of the allegorical interpretations were less favourable to women than literal ones.

One of the most striking and perhaps shocking attempts at an allegorical interpretation of male-female imagery in the Bible is presented by the Jewish philosopher of the early Patristic period, Philo of Alexandria.[4] According to Philo, the story of the creation of Adam and Eve and the fall into sin are to be interpreted allegorically in terms of the idea that the male principle, Adam, represents mind and the female principle, Eve, represents sense experience. On this reading, the period before Eve was created is the time in which the mind, Adam, reigns supreme, being purely rational and dedicated to God. With the creation of the feminine, Eve, the realm of sense experience is born. The fall into sin, caused by Eve giving the fruit to Adam, means that the pure mind is defiled by sense experience. This means that the mind is opened up to the temptations of the world, that is, to desires which are aroused by the information which comes to man through the five senses. These are desires such as the sexual drive, gluttony, and the greed for earthly things and material goods. Man is thus removed from the pure contemplation of God and hence becomes sinful. Woven into this allegory of the feminine as sense experience is Philo's conception of women as temptresses who lead men away from the straight and narrow path. The feminine, Philo says, expresses mankind's lower nature.

In the mainstream of Judeo-Christian theological thought, a view of women such as that of Philo was rejected. A certain consensus about how to view women arose. A number of conclusions emerged from these medieval debates, conclusions which form the general theological outline of a view of women in Christian churches to this day. Traditionally, the role of the woman is seen to be in the home, oriented to her husband, children and family. Women are to obey and remain subservient to men both in marriage and in the Church since they are in some sense inferior to men. Women are, however, considered to have souls and rationality by virtue of the fact that they are human beings. Celibacy is seen as a state which has more perfection than marriage, but on the other hand, marriage is necessary for containing sexual desires within a proper context and for the purpose of reproduction.

Much of the complexity of the medieval discussions has been forgotten, yet the interpretations developed at this time have had an extraordinarily long lifespan. In this chapter, I shall discuss some of the views of St. Thomas Aquinas on women. I will first deal with Aquinas' interpretation of the story of creation and the fall into sin as related in Genesis. In these passages, St. Thomas Aquinas is influenced by Aristotle's biology, discussed in the previous chapter. In the second part of this chapter, I will deal with Aquinas' interpretation of the New Testament texts concerning the role of women in the Church, their rationality and spirituality. I will attempt to show that his interpretation of Biblical passages concerning women in the Church is consistent with and related to his view of the way he believes God created women. In the next chapter, I will discuss a feminine reaction to such theologically based views of women by showing how Christine de Pizan argues for a completely different attitude and approach to this question.

2   The Creation of Woman

St. Thomas Aquinas writes in a formal, medieval style. First, he presents what he calls a Question. This question is subdivided into articles. In the articles, different sub-themes of the question are discussed. He begins the article by presenting the views of philosophers and theologians with whom he does not agree. These views are called Objections. After stating a number of these objections, he writes the words "On the contrary". Under this heading, he summarises his own position. Then, after the words "I answer that", he presents a more detailed statement of his views. Finally, there is a heading "Reply" to the objections mentioned at the beginning, in which he rejects the views he does not agree with point by point. This style can be somewhat confusing because of its complexity. I will, however, in my discussion of the questions I have chosen, follow quite closely the construction of Aquinas' writing. In order to help the reader follow the complicated progress of Aquinas' arguments, I will indicate at what point of the question we are. In keeping with Aquinas' own debating style, I will not only present his views but I will make some objections to his views and suggestions for alternative ways of seeing the matters being discussed.

In Questions 92 and 93 of the *Summa Theologica*, St. Thomas Aquinas (1225-1274) deals with issues surrounding the creation and nature of man and woman.[5] Question 92 deals with "The Production of Woman". In the first article of question 92, he considers the question, "Whether the woman should have been made in the first production of things?". This question arises because there was a perfect state in paradise before the fall into sin. Should woman have been made at this perfect stage as the Bible relates? He considers three possible Objections which theologians of his time might have to accepting the idea that woman should have been present in paradise. The first objection Aquinas mentions is based on Aristotle's idea that women are "misbegotten males" and hence are defective creatures, unworthy of existing in paradise. The second objection which he notes is based on Augustine's idea that women, as "patients" are subjected to men as "agents" (again,

Aristotelian terms), and are therefore less perfect than men and, again, had no right to be in paradise. The third objection concerns the point that since woman, Eve, caused Adam and then the world to fall into sin, women should not have been created in the first place. *Ergo*, there should have been only males in paradise.

Aquinas' Answer to these objections is that God created woman to be in paradise and that this was right. It was necessary for God to create women in the perfect state before the fall into sin because woman was meant to be a helper for man. Woman was created as a helper for man, not in other works, for in those a man is better helped by another man (Aristotle) but woman is a helper in the "work of generation", that is, reproduction. Following Aristotle, he says that "Wherefore we observe that in these the active power of generation invariably accompanies the passive power. Among perfect animals the active power of generation belongs to the male sex, and the passive to the female". The justification for Eve being in paradise is therefore her role as passive accompaniment to the active male gender.

Aquinas then proceeds to state that although women were made for the purpose of reproduction, the male is not in "continual union" with the female. In keeping with Aristotle's view on this matter, he states: "But man is yet further ordered to a still nobler vital action, and that is intellectual operation. Therefore there was greater reason for the distinction between these two forces in man; so that the female should be produced separately from the male; although they are carnally united for generation. Therefore directly after the formation of woman, it was said: *And they shall be two in one flesh* (Gen. 2:24)."

Although St. Thomas Aquinas attacks the Objections that woman had no right to be in paradise, his own views as expressed in the Answer summarised above, leave something to be desired. I will therefore now formulate *my* objections to *his* view. In his statement concerning the reason why it was necessary to have women in paradise, he bases himself on the Biblical description of Eve as the "helper" of Adam. He interprets the term "helper" as referring solely to the activity of reproduction, thereby firmly referring women to their biological function as their only justification for being and their only real purpose in life. This is the Aristotelian use of this word, but is such an interpretation justified on Biblical grounds?

I would suggest that one could object that St. Thomas Aquinas' position here is indeed debatable because of the way in which he misinterprets the word "helper". The Hebrew word used in this text is also found in another book of the Bible, the Psalms. There God is called our "Help".[6] This usage does not refer to the notions of reproduction or of inferiority, but connotes matters such as standing by one's side, supporting one another, being there for one another. Since the context of the use of this word in Genesis is Adam's feeling of loneliness at not having a mate as all the animals do, this would seem to be a more likely meaning of the term.[7]

Secondly, one could object to St. Thomas Aquinas' acceptance of Aristotelian ideas such as the systematics of active (superior) and passive (inferior) powers of generation to distinguish between the male and female task in generation. Perhaps knowledge of biology was not very advanced in Aquinas' time, but there seems to be little justification for linking male domination of women to their mysterious "active power of generation". Furthermore, the idea that men should only associate with women for reproductive purposes because they have intellectual tasks to do is manifestly absurd: witness Aquinas's statement that men have "a still nobler vital action, and that is intellectual operation" as opposed to the presumed inactivity of women in this area. When he finally concludes that the purpose of male and female is that "they shall be two in one flesh", this must be read in the context of women having primarily a reproductive task in life and of male superiority over women.

We are now at the point at which Aquinas, in light of the Answer given above, gives Replies to the Objections to the idea of woman being in paradise with which the article started. There were three objections mentioned. I will go through Aquinas' replies to each one.

In his answer to the first objection, Aquinas *agrees* with the position that woman is misbegotten in her individual nature but not in terms of the "general intention of nature" which is "directed to the work of generation". That is, as an individual person she is not perfect, as the male is, but she has her own type of perfection within the whole context of nature, that is, for the purpose of reproduction.

In his reply to the second objection, Aquinas *agrees* both with Aristotle and the Christian tradition that female subjection is proper because there is always subjection among people. It is right for women to be ruled by men, for men have more rationality than women, he argues. Subjection is thus not a fault in creation, but it is a matter of proper order.

Replying to the third objection, Aquinas states that, since it was necessary to create woman, God did not make the mistake of creating someone who would cause sin to come into the world. God created the common good as good, and besides, he adds, God can direct any evil to a good end.

I would now like to make some comments on the way in which Aquinas responds to the Objections. In his response to the first objection, Aquinas concedes Aristotle's point that women are defective and misbegotten, but that she is needed for the whole order of things. There is, as far as I know, no mention in the Bible of the idea that a woman is defective or misbegotten, a not insignificant problem in Aquinas' argument. As was mentioned in the discussion of the passages of *De Generatione Animalium* in the chapter on Aristotle, the idea of the woman as misbegotten is based on a biological misconception on the part of Aristotle. Aristotle believed that only the male provided the "form" for the child, the female provided the "matter", that is, the material nurturing of the child in the womb. Since deviation from "form" means, biologically speaking, having defects (for example, a child born without certain limbs or organs is defective), women, in not resembling their formal originators, men, are seen as defective males. Once more, we have the problem here of Aquinas using ideas which are biologically inaccurate in order to justify male superiority over females.

In Aquinas' reply to the second objection, he states that there are different aspects to the subjection of women. He states that there is no servile subjection before the fall into sin, but that there is always in any state an element of subjection: he mentions economic and civic forms of subjection as examples. In other words, there is a bad (servile) and good form of subjection, based on the right order of things. Between men and women, this proper form of subjection is based on the fact that men are "wiser" and "in man the discretion of reason predominates". Apart from the unfounded claim that males have more reason than females, there is also again in this case a matter of theological dispute about the accuracy of Aquinas' argument.

Aquinas, as we have seen, argues that the subjection of women to men is a good and normal matter, part of the general order of things. On what grounds is this argument based? There is no indication in the passage of Genesis here being discussed that Eve was subjected to Adam. The notion of the subjection of the female to the male is introduced in Genesis 3. Here it does not refer to the state of paradise but is introduced in the context of the curses which befell women as a result of the fall into sin. The curse of subjection is mentioned together with a number of other curses: for woman, bearing children in pain, for man, tilling the ground, working hard, and, for both, eventually death. These curses are not particularly attractive, hence one can object to Aquinas that not only was there no question of women being inferior to men in paradise, resulting in the "proper" subjection of women to men in that state, but that there are, contrary to his claim, no sinless forms of subjection of women. Subjection is precisely a result of sin, according to the Biblical account. The fact that mankind has been actively reducing the impact of the curses in Genesis 3 (lengthening lifespan, reducing labour pains, lightening work loads) would seem to point to a more liberal interpretation of the subjection of women: that it is time to deal with that curse as well. Aquinas' interpretation, in not going down this road, articulates a more secular reality, the factual subjection of women in his society. Putting this argument in a more theological mode, Aquinas here fails to take into consideration the liberating aspects of the Bible as the history of redemption and of the way people have dealt with the curses placed on them, ideas which he does introduce elsewhere in his theology.[8]

In his reply to the third objection, Aquinas states that even though women are an "occasion to sin", they are properly created by God for a common good, and that God can turn all evil to a good end. This argument resembles Aristotle's position that woman was created to serve a greater good, reproduction, and that one should regard her in that perspective. One can object to Aquinas' use of this view that women are not totally responsible for the fall into sin. Adam too sinned by eating of the forbidden fruit and to emphasise that, creation only fell into sin when *he* acted contrary to God's commandments.

Aquinas' views as presented here have had a strong influence on western theology. We can still recognise some of the ideas put forward here. That women exist mainly for the purpose of reproduction has been the position of the Church for centuries. In addition, the notion that men are more perfect, active, intelligent and wise can and has been used to justify male rule within the Church.

In the second article of Question 92, the question raised is whether woman should have been made from man, as the creation story in the Bible relates. This question arises because, as is stated in Objection 1, it seems unnatural that a female would come into being from a male. Objection 2 states that it seems unnatural that people of the same species are not made from the same material: that is, Adam was made from clay or slime, while Eve was made from a different material, Adam's rib; Objection 3 states that if Eve was created from out of Adam's rib she would be so closely related to him that they should not have had a sexual relationship or children.

Aquinas, in his reply to these Objections, states that God made Eve out of Adam. In his Answer to the objections, he makes a number of points. Firstly, Eve, the woman, was made from Adam, the man, in order to give Adam dignity as the "first principle" of the human race just as God is the first principle of the universe. Hence Eve's creation out of Adam is an affirmation of Adam's supreme human status. Secondly, Aquinas argues that God's making woman out of a part of the body of the man means that the two are of the same nature, they are to "cleave together", that is, spend their lives together in marriage. Thirdly, Aquinas argues that woman was made out of man to symbolise "...domestic life...in which the man is the head of the woman". His "headship" is based on and symbolised by the fact that the man is the "origin" or "principle" of woman. Finally, Aquinas states that woman was created out of man in order to symbolise the sacramental meaning of the fact that the Church has her origin in Christ just as Eve has her origin in Adam.

I would like to *respond* to this Answer of St. Thomas Aquinas. Although this article contains discussions which are not all that pressing in our time from a theological or social point of view, a number of assumptions and assertions about women are here being made which reveal deeply embedded prejudices about women.

The first point which Aquinas makes in his answer is to say that the creation of Eve from out of Adam is a confirmation of Adam's position as male, image of God, and principle of the human race. One could object that God created Eve out of Adam, but that that does not necessarily mean he now has greater status as "principle of the human race". If Aquinas were consistent here, he would again refer to Aristotle's view that the material cause of generation is not the formal cause. In other words, when women provide the material for generation this seems to justify their inferiority, when men provide the material, it turns them into a "first principle". Women's contribution to the origin of man does not seem to have had much effect on her status; a man's contribution affirms his superiority. "Origin", apparently, does not *as such* guarantee primacy, unless one has already decided the question of primacy beforehand and on grounds external to the argument being presented. Aquinas does point out that Adam's material is used by God to create Eve. Adam is not of course her father. But this remark by Aquinas muddles the argument concerning the male being the principle of the human race even further.

In the second and third points in Aquinas' answer he argues on the one hand that the creation of Eve from out of Adam means that they are to be united, to be one, to cleave together in monogamous marriage. On the other hand, however, the creation of Eve out of Adam does not mean, for Aquinas, the equality of these two halves. He reiterates his position that man is the head of woman and of the household. Here one can introduce the same objections to Aquinas' position as were mentioned earlier in the discussion of Aquinas' notion of the subjection of women to men as already having taken place in paradise.

Finally, Aquinas argues that there is a "sacramental reason" for the creation of Eve. Just as the Church takes her origin in Christ, so woman has her origin in man. I will return to this point at the end of this chapter when I will discuss imagery relating to women and the Church.

In the final two articles of Question 92, dealing with the creation of woman, Aquinas first considers the Question and Objections to the issue of whether woman was made from the rib of man and secondly whether she was formed immediately by God or by other causes, such as man, angels or causes within creation itself.

In his Answer to the question of whether woman was made out of the rib of man, Aquinas states:

> *I answer that*, It was right for the woman to be made from a rib of man. First, to signify the social union of man and woman, for the woman should neither *use authority over man*, and so she was not made from his head; nor was it right for her to be subject to man's contempt as his slave, and so she was not made from his feet. Secondly, for the sacramental signification; for from the side of

Christ sleeping on the Cross the Sacraments flowed – namely, blood and water – on which the Church was established.[9]

Aquinas here restates his view that there is a hierarchical relationship between men and women. A woman must not have authority over a man but at the same time she is not his slave. One could object to this by referring back to the original question of whether Eve should have been made from Adam. Aquinas, as we saw, argued that this was indeed so. But this means that Eve is made from a higher type of material than Adam himself was. Is this not a relevant point to consider? If one sees the process of creation as a process of continuing completion and perfection in the course of 6 days, as Aquinas does, then it is logical that Eve comes out of a higher type of material than Adam. It would be less logical to have an idea of creation coming to its epitomy in the creation of the male, taking a down turn at the creation of the female, the last being created, a "necessarily lower" afterthought. Already in the Middle Ages, Hildegard von Bingen, a German mystic, discussed this point and considered the possibility that perhaps woman, not man, is the highest creature made by God.

According to Aquinas, woman should be neither the head nor the slave of man, yet for all that she should be subservient to man. One may, spuriously, consider the fact that man does not come from woman's head or feet either and ask what this implies in terms of male authority over women.

Aquinas here affirms the hierarchical order between the two genders. Such a position is quite typical of a Judeo-Christian theological view of women in that it combines complementarity with hierarchy. Summarizing responses to such a view, one can attempt to solve this double attitude towards women in various ways. Firstly, it is possible to try to reverse the hierarchical order, that is, by pointing out that women can very well be seen as the final and highest product of creation: there is no real reason why it should have been men. Secondly, one can focus on the complementarity aspect of this view of women and emphasise that it affirms equality. Then Aquinas' most fundamental presupposition underlying his response is simply that of the bias that men are superior to women. Lastly, one can also attack the attempt as such to make distinctions between men and women "before God".

Next, Aquinas deals with the problem of the precise material from out of which Eve was made. Here he once more appeals to the power of God:

> Now God alone, the Author of nature, can produce an effect into existence outside the ordinary course of nature. Therefore God alone could produce either a man from the slime of the earth, or a woman from the rib of man.[10]

Aquinas replies to the objections that they should take into account the Divine Power to perform an act of creation. Ultimately, it was God who created Eve, hence Eve was not the daughter of Adam.

3 Woman as the Image of God

I would now like to turn to the next question, Question 93, which deals with "The end or term of the production of man". I would like to discuss the fourth article of this question, in which the question is posed, "Whether the image of God is found in every man?"

In this article, St. Thomas Aquinas is dealing with a question debated more often in the Middle Ages, whether all men are created in the image of God and whether women are or are not made in His image. He first considers the following Objections. Firstly, women, although part of the human species, are nevertheless not made in the image of God. Only man is because "man is the image of God, but woman is the image (glory) of man". The second objection is that some people are chosen by God to be made in his image (predestination) and others are not. Thirdly, it is argued that no man is the image of God because all people are sinful.

Aquinas' Answer is that man is the image of God. This is so primarily by virtue of his intellect. He notes three ways in which man is the image of God: firstly, through his intellect which gives him a "natural aptitude" for loving and understanding God; secondly, since God has both love and intellect in Himself, man is his image in grace before God; and thirdly, man is the image of God because he is created in His image, can re-create His image, and, in the case of the blessed, he can be a likeness of God. In his replies to the three objections mentioned above,

Aquinas considers the issue of whether women too are made in the image of God.

In his response to the first objection, he states that both men and women have an intellectual nature and therefore both are made in the image of God in the "primary" sense. But in the so-called "secondary" sense, Aquinas adds, man is made in the image of God and woman is not. Aquinas states that, quoting Paul, "man is the image and glory of God, but woman is the glory of man...For man is not of woman, but woman of man; and man was not created for woman, but woman for man". Once again, Adam is more "primary" and closer to God than woman because of the idea mentioned earlier that man is the origin and the principle of the human race through Adam.

One can make several objections to Aquinas' distinction between a primary and secondary sense in which woman is and is not the image of God. The position he takes here can be called one of "spiritual equality and natural subordination", that is, in the spiritual, primary sense, woman is equal to man and is made in the image of God, but in terms of the natural order, that is, the male-female relationship, man is in the image of God and woman is so only in a secondary sense." The duality of spiritual equality and natural subordination is deeply embedded in the Christian tradition. As such, it is not a completely consistent position to take. If, from out of the perspective of God men and women are to be seen in terms of His image, then why, when women are regarded in terms of their relationship to men are they placed on a secondary plane? This means that somehow the position men have determines the place of women, but God's position does not have any effect on the place of women. Since God seems to be rather more important than males, this seems at least on first sight a curious view to hold. Aquinas, as we saw when discussing the previous question, however, does not consider this view to be unusual in that the order of nature demands subordination.

The idea that women are not the image of God in the secondary sense is related to ideas, mentioned in Questions 92 and 93, concerning the role of Eve as mother of the human race. As we saw, Adam is the principle of the human race. Woman was created for man, not man for woman. We saw, however, that Aquinas holds that woman was created out of man as an act of God, but not of man himself (thus avoiding the problems of too close a genetic relationship between the two). Over against this, one might consider the notion that woman has always, at least after the creation, been the origin of man. That is according to Aquinas precisely her value in creation, as we saw when considering Question 92, article 1. Once more, a view of Hildegard von Bingen, the medieval mystic, can perhaps provide an alternative. She argues that women are the origin of the human race and have the primary power of reproduction. She even attributes the fall into sin to this characteristic of women: Satan tempted Eve because he was jealous of her reproductive powers.[12]

In these particular articles by Aquinas concerning women, it is obvious from the terminology used that ideas of Aristotle were of influence on his views, mixed together with theological ideas taken from the Bible and the Christian tradition, with, in the background, deeply held social-cultural convictions concerning men and women. As has been shown, there are a number of assumptions and assertions which can be debated, both in terms of the compatibility of Aristotle's views with those of the Bible as well as in terms of Aquinas' interpretation of the Bible passages mentioned.

4   Aquinas' View of Women in the Church

There are several implications of the hierarchical view of the nature of women, implications which have had an inestimable impact on the view of women and their role in society in western culture. This impact has been greatest in three areas: in marriage, with respect to job opportunities and in the Church itself. As a result of a view of women such as the one which Aquinas distills from Genesis, women are to be subservient to men in marriage, are not to have authority over men within society and have a secondary role to play in the Church. I would now like to turn to Aquinas' view of women in the Church.[13] Aquinas is consistent in his interpretation of the implications of Genesis for the nature of women and his interpretation of New Testament passages on their role in the Church. Aquinas discusses a number of New Testament texts referring to women, in particular texts written by St. Paul. There are several issues which he discusses.

Following the Pauline guidelines, Aquinas considers it improper for women to have their heads uncovered (1 Corinthians 11:3-15) and to speak in Church (1 Corinthians 14:34-35). Men, on the other hand, can do both. This is based, as we saw earlier, on the notion of the man being the image of God in a primary sense, the woman not.

Central to his views is his interpretation of the allegory of the Church as the Bride of Christ (Ephesians 5:21-33). The concept of the bride is that she is faithful, loving, and subservient to her husband (1 Peter 3:1; Collosians 3:18). In this sense, the Church is the Bride of Christ. Transferring this to the allegorical mode, this means that the Church, with men in the dominant role, is to have a female role towards Christ. Men thus have a female role towards Christ, and women have a female role both towards men and to Christ on a higher plane. This is a mixed metaphor which, on one level, makes sense, on another it does not.[14] The metaphor begins to strain when the bride-bridegroom imagery is repeated on the concrete male-female level within the Church itself. For, are not all the members of the Church female in relation to Christ? Why then distinguish within the Church between men and women?

The image of man-woman, Christ-Church, is prevalent in Christian theology and gives rise to a number of points and arguments. It has been used as a powerful argument to justify male rule over women in the Church because it introduces suprahuman or divine reasons for female subjugation. But on the suggested alternative interpretation of this image it means that there is no justification for a male hierarchical structure *within* the Church, for, as was stated, everyone in the Church is equally the Bride of Christ. Admittedly, however, the image does seem to justify a hierarchical structure *outside* the Church, specifically in marriage.

With respect to women, marriage and subservience within the Church, Aquinas makes a distinction between married and unmarried women. An unmarried woman does not participate in the "bride" role in the same way as a married woman, who must be subservient to her husband. Her subservience to men is placed within the context of the Church and not her husband.[15] But, on the other hand, married and unmarried women entering into religious orders are still subservient to male supervision of that order.

A text which might be able to liberate women from all these hierarchies based on gender would seem to be Galations 3:28 where it is stated that there is no male and no female in Christ. This would seem to imply that the spiritual life is neutral with regard to gender. Aquinas, in commenting on this text, however, claims that the text refers only to the next life in which there will be no more distinction made, but that in this life the distinction still applies.[16]

5   Theoretical Contexts for Interpreting Aquinas' View of Women

A number of theoretical contexts have been suggested in the literature to give a wider perspective on Aquinas' view on women. I shall here present two approaches which I think are innovative and interesting.

Firstly, I would like to return to the notion mentioned earlier, that of "spiritual equality and natural subordination". "Spiritual equality" refers to the idea in Christianity that men and women are equal before God. Both are called to the faith, are capable of religious feeling and action, have equal chances of attaining salvation, are both human in the sense that they have reason and are created in the image of God. This means that on the spiritual level, both genders have enough spiritual and rational ability to understand the contents of Christian doctrine and its implications in personal and social terms.

It has been argued that in this sense, Christianity improved the image and position of women, in contrast to the way the Greeks thought about them. While perhaps in some forms of Greek thought doubts were cast on the heights which women could reach with their emotional and rational powers, this no longer seems possible in Christian thought.

In contrast to this optimistic interpretation, it has also been argued that the concept of "spiritual equality" is a limited one. As C. Capelle, in an exceedingly thorough book shows, it is unclear whether Aquinas truly considered men and women to be equally rational: some passages indicate that he thought this, others that he did not.[17] In addition, the notion of equal spiritual emotionality and insight seems undermined by the fact that Aquinas insists on the fact that women must be subservient to men in the faith, symbolised most clearly by the fact that they are not allowed to perform the priestly sacramental functions.

Women are thus in a sense spiritually equal to men, but not entirely so. Contrasted to and related to the concept of "spiritual equality" is the notion of "natural subordination". Natural subordination refers to the human, everyday realm of life, in which concrete phenomena such as gender play a role. Natural subordination refers to the hierarchical structure in this world, the rule of the higher over the lower in all spheres.

But it is not at all easy to distinguish between the realms of spiritual equality and natural subordination or, for that matter, to keep them apart. As we have asked before, if people are equal before God, why are they unequal among themselves? This question is also raised by Aquinas and has, of course, bothered the Church for millennia, not only in terms of male-female distinctions but also in terms of the social concerns of the Church in general. Aquinas, as we saw, makes use of Aristotle's idea that there is a proper order for the general good. Women, however, have not been convinced that their subordinate role is for the general good and would, I think, tend to believe that such ordering of male superiority over against female subservience is rather too "natural" a male impulse. To what extent is the concept of natural subordination a theoretical or theological notion and to what extent is it a rationalisation of necessities, needs, instincts or desires? Or is this concept actually an expression of the incapacity of human beings to create a world with justice and equality for all?

A second context within which Aquinas can be read is a rather more sympathetic one in the sense that it can be argued that Aquinas is mirroring existing social relationships and conventions in his philosophy and theology. Hence, reading his views in a historical context, they should be judged as reflections of his time. C. Capelle, in her study of Aquinas' view of women, tends to some extent towards this type of interpretation, yet for all that, she does note that if one looks at the historical dimension, one should also consider the eschatological one. In other words, even if one glosses over Aquinas' views as the reflection of views of his time, as a theologian, Aquinas should have been aware of the Biblical view of history. The Bible tells a history of people and their faith. It speaks of a movement towards greater revelation and realisation of God's purpose of earth. There is very little dynamism in Aquinas' views, that is, a forward looking element pointing towards a perspective of liberation. As in the case of Aristotle, gender roles are set and not seen as subject to alteration in different historical periods or societies.

Capelle argues that if an eschatological perspective were built into Aquinas' views, it would offer more openness to women. Her book moreover indicates that the medievals were aware of changes in the view and place of women in history and in different societies. They were aware of the fact that in the Bible there are indications of changes from, for example, a polygamous society to a monogamous one, from allowing divorce to forbidding it. I think that the eschatological approach is an interesting one in that it both allows for the fact that Aquinas reflected the views of his time and yet presents him with the issue of how to approach the problem of the analysis of the nature and roles of women in a historical setting.

In the next chapter, I will deal with the protest of the late medieval – early Renaissance writer, historian, poet and philosopher Christine de Pizan against images of women which fail to do justice to their courage, intelligence, strength and faith. Unlike St. Thomas Aquinas, Christine de Pizan places the question of images of women within a truly wonderful eschatological perspective of rehabilitation and liberation. She argues that women, with the help of God Himself, will overcome the injustice which has been done to them.

Notes

1   Augustine's answer, by the way, is that Adam and Eve had sexual contact without arousal: this is now no longer possible after the fall into sin, but before that, it was a miracle of God. For a detailed discussion of these questions, see: Rosemary Radford Ruether, "Misogynism and Virginal Feminism in the Fathers of the Church", in: R. Radford Ruether, ed. *Religion and Sexism*. New York, Simon and Schuster, 1974, p. 150-183.

2   Eleanor Commo McLaughlin, "Equality of Souls, Inequality of Sexes: Woman in Medieval Theology", in: Rosemary Radford Reuther, ed., *Religion and Sexism*. New York, Simon and Schuster, 1974, p. 233-245.

3   See for example, St. Augustine, *The Literal Meaning of Genesis*, Vol. I and II. In the series: *Ancient Christian Writers*, Vol. 41 and 42. transl. by J.H. Taylor. New York, Newman Press, 1982.

4   Philo of Alexandria, *Complete Works*. transl. by H. Colson and H. Whitaker. Loeb Classical Library, 1952. See for example: Part I, *On the Creation*, 148-171, LIII-LIX, p. 119-239; *Allegorical Interpretation* II, 11-53, p. 233-257, and 73-78, p. 271-273, and 98-103, p. 287-289; *Allegorical Interpretation* III, 9-15, p. 307-309 and 199-227, p. 437-455; Part II, *On the Cherubim*, 6-19, p. 13-19; *The Worse Attacks the Better*, 27-30, p. 221;

101-109, p. 271-275; Part III, *The Special Laws* I, 195-204, p. 213-215, *The Special Laws* III, 166-182, p. 581-589.

5 St. Thomas Aquinas, *Summa Theologica*. Part I. transl. by the Fathers of the Dominican Province. London, Burns, Oates and Washbourne, 1911. Vol. 4, p. 274-278 and p. 288-289.

6 See Genesis 2:20 and Psalm 124.

7 I owe this idea to the pioneering Dutch feminist, Mrs. Diemer-Lindeboom. An interview with her on feminism and faith can be found in *Beweging* 48 (1984, 6).

8 For a detailed discussion of this objection and the notion of history and eschatology in Aquinas' work, see C. Capelle, *Thomas d'Aquin féministe?*, Paris, Vrin, 1982, p. 167-171.

9 St. Thomas Aquinas, *Summa Theologica*. Part I. transl. by the Fathers of the Dominican Province. London, Burns, Oates and Washbourne, 1911. Vol. 4, p. 279.

10 St. Thomas Aquinas, *Summa Theologica*. Part I. transl. by the Fathers of the English Dominican Province. London, Burns, Oates and Washbourne, 1911. Vol. 4, p. 281.

11 This type of analysis is given by G. Lloyd, *The Man of Reason*, London, Methuen, 1984, p. 28-37.

12 Hildegard von Bingen, *Welt und Mensch*. ed. by Heinrich Schipperges. Salzburg, Otto Müller Verlag, 1965, p. 202-203.

13 My choice of this topic is now all the more important to me as an expression of protest against various recent decisions in mainstream Christian churches to reaffirm the ban on women in office.

14 C. Capelle, *Thomas d'Aquin féministe?*, Paris, Vrin, 1982, p.153-162.

15 C. Capelle, *Thomas d'Aquin Féministe?*, Paris, Vrin, 1982, p. 155, 161.

16 C. Capelle, *Thomas d'Aquin Féministe?*, Paris, Vrin, 1982, p. 116, 126.

17 C. Capelle, *Thomas d'Aquin féministe?*, Paris, Vrin, 1982, p. 61.

5 Christine de Pizan. The Feminine Response

1 Introduction.

This book opened with the Pythagorean women speaking about their role in the home and expressing ideals of female virtues. I would like to close off the discussion of the ancient and medieval period as well as open the way to modernity with another female voice, that of Christine de Pizan. I will begin by contrasting Christine's view of women with that of St. Thomas Aquinas. Then I will turn to Christine's view of an alternative history of women which is written with the desire to radically change views of women in light of the principle, as it was stated in Descartes' philosophy later, of thinking and reasoning for oneself, not purely out of tradition.

Christine de Pizan (1364-1430) was a poet, novelist, historian and philosopher. Born in Venice, Italy, her father, Thomas de Pizan, was a government official. He later received the job of adviser to King Charles V of France and after three years the family moved to Paris to join him there in 1369. Christine, married in 1379 at age fifteen to Etienne de Castel, had three children and was widowed in 1389 when her husband died of the plague. She was then twenty-five. Her father had passed away as well, and Christine, her mother and her children had a hard time making ends meet. She had legal problems as well, concerning money matters, but, as she protests, women were unable to go to court to defend themselves and present their case. After fourteen years of litigation these problems subsided, and Christine was making a living by writing.[1]

2 Literature and Mythology as Allegory

We have seen how powerfully the traditional image of women was supported and strengthened with arguments by Aristotle and St. Thomas Aquinas. These two thinkers had a great deal of influence not only because of the persuasive arguments with which they placed women within the familial and reproductive order but also because their views were sanctioned by the authority of Christian theology.

Christine de Pizan realised that if she were to deal with the negative views of women which she considered to be prevalent in her society and time, she must deal with the theological context of such views. She was not a theologian, nor was she concerned with presenting a feminist theology in the modern sense of the word. A feminist theology would attempt to attack Bible interpretations which lead to a negative view of women by means of a traditional scholarly method. Christine instead puts her literary skills into the battle and writes a feminine allegory, based on a Bible story. As such, this approach is very effective indeed. The result is a critique which does not enter the literal battleground but rises above it as an inspiration. Christine demonstrates by her artistry that there are effective ways with which to attack chauvenism and to give women new perspectives on themselves. Christine presents her alternative view of women in the *Book of The City of Ladies*. The title of the book refers to the City of God, spoken of at the end of the Bible book Revelation. According to the Bible story, after the last plagues are cast over the earth, the end of the world has come, and the last judgment has taken place, a city descends from heaven. This is the new Jerusalem and in it can enter only those whose names are written in the book of life. The city has no suffering in it and no day or night, for there is always light in it. God is its light, and Christ, its lamp, rule the city.

In the Biblical account, the construction of the city has a symbolical significance. The city has a radiance like a jasper and a clarity as crystal. It has high walls and is square, having in total twelve gates, three gates on each side. On the gates are inscribed the names of the twelve tribes of Israel. The wall of the city has twelve foundations, with written on them the names of the twelve apostles of Christ. The number twelve and its square, one hundred and fourty-four, are the proportions of the length and area measurements of the city. These numbers symbolise perfection and point to those who may enter the city: the spiritual descendents of the twelve tribes and the twelve apostles. The city is made entirely of precious metals and stones. The gates are each made of a single pearl.[2] The Bible story already contains symbolism; Christine de Pizan uses symbolism as well but transforms its content and direction.

In the Bible story, the city is allegorically called the Bride, the wife of Christ. Christine de Pizan also imagines a city, but it is not only symbolically female but is specifically meant for real-life women. Instead of the male names found on the walls and foundations, Christine imagines that the foundations are formed by courageous women, the walls by the wise, and the buildings by the pious. For Christine, the most noble women are found in the third category; they are the saints and martyrs, those who were courageous and persistent in the faith. As Christine writes:

> We must lodge holy women with the Blessed Virgin – the holy Queen of Heaven, Empress and Princess of the City of Ladies – to keep her company and to demonstrate God's approval of the feminine sex with examples of His giving young and tender women (just as he has done with men) the constancy and strength to suffer horrible martyrdom for His holy law, women who are crowned in glory and whose fair lives serve as excellent examples for every woman above all other wisdom. For this reason these women are the most outstanding of our City.[3]

Hence she appeals to Mary, the mother of Christ, to come and take her place as the ruler of the city. Christine thus replaces the masculine symbols of the Bible story with feminine ones.

Christine's setting of this allegory is also allegorical: she herself is to "build" the city. Her book opens with an account of herself sitting at her writing table, feeling saddened by all the negative things which have been said throughout the ages about women. Suddenly three women appear to her. They explain to her that they are the allegorical figures of Reason, Rectitude and Justice. These are the three weapons needed in the battle against sexism. Prejudices against women can only be taken away by thinking about women in a rational way, in seeing them in the right light and in being fair when judging women.

The three figures are presented in an evocative way. On the one hand, they resemble Greek inspirational muses. After all, Christine is supposed to be inspired by them to write an attack on sexism, girded by the strength of the values these women represent. On the other hand, these allegorical figures can be associated with the Christian notion of angels as messengers of God. Christine herself calls the women Ladies and, even more tellingly, describes them as daughters of God. By the respect she shows the Ladies and her description of them as living in the presence of God, she implies that Reason, Rectitude and Justice are characteristics of God Himself. She does not hesitate to represent these characteristics of God as feminine.

The women command Christine to build the city of women. The ground must be prepared, foundations laid, mortar and bricks, the material from out of which the city is to be built, be gathered and cemented together. These steps in the construction of the city refer to the material which Christine is to use to demonstrate the good qualities of outstanding women. The purpose of the book is to document all the courage, wisdom and piety of women from ancient times onwards. Christine includes many ancient legends, Greek mythology, Bible stories and historical material to make her case on behalf of women. Christine states that her purpose is to clear women of all the bad things that have been said about them and to inspire other women to achieve the things their great predecessors have done. Christine thus uses her material in a surprisingly modern way: to rediscover and rewrite feminine history.

3   Alternative Images of Women

In her *Book of the City of Ladies*, Christine de Pizan's main aim is to find different patterns, formulate different notions, of the nature of women and their capacities. She thus expresses a very fundamental desire of women: to alter the way in which they think about themselves and how others see them. To illustrate this, I will discuss one example taken from each of the three categories in which Christine describes women: the example I have chosen from the category of courageous women is that of the Amazons, of wise women, Minerva, and of pious women, St. Catherine.

Christine de Pizan mentions the Amazons at the beginning of her book, placing the stories she tells about them in the category of stones which are placed in the trenches dug to contain the foundations of the City of Ladies. They belong to the foundations because they are proof of the fact that women are as strong, courageous, determined and warlike as men.[4]

Christine relates that the Amazons lived in Scythia, a land located on the edge of the great Ocean which surrounds the entire world. Long ago, all the males of fighting age were killed off in warfare, leaving only women, elderly men and children in the land. The women decided that they would run their country themselves and they banned all men from their territory. The women went to neighbouring countries at certain times of the year in order to conceive children. They returned pregnant to their country and when they bore male children, they would send them back to their fathers, keeping their female children themselves.

Next, they formed a kingdom with two queens at the head, Lampheto and Marthesie, and proceeded to create a strong army with which they attacked their enemies. The Amazons owed their name, "without a breast" to the fact that they would cut off one breast in order to be able to weild a shield (left breast) or a bow (right breast).

Christine relates at length the military exploits of the Amazons, claiming that their power lasted for eight hundred years, up to the time of the conquests of Alexander the Great. They captured neighbouring countries, gaining enormous wealth and a fearsome reputation. They ambushed, defeated and killed Cyrus, King of Persia, and his army when they invaded their country. In turn Hercules and Theseus, King of Athens, decided to invade. They thought that the Amazons were such a risk to Greek security that a pre-emptive strike would be a good idea. The result of this encounter was a truce between the Amazons and the Greeks. Later, however, the Amazons supported the Trojans in their fight against the Greeks, wishing to revenge the death of Hector at the hands of Achilles.

Reading the stories Christine de Pizan relates about the Amazons, different people may react in different ways. For Christine and many of her readers, the message of these stories is a positive one: it shows that the Amazon women are physically and mentally strong, independent, and courageous. In some readers, these stories may arouse a feeling of dismay at the fact that women are being described as having characteristics which at times resemble arguably the worst traits in men.

The most telling example of this issue is the story of the Amazonian Queen Tomyris and King Cyrus. Tomyris hated Cyrus so much that she had him and his nobles taken prisoner, had the nobles beheaded before Cyrus' own eyes, beheaded Cyrus and threw his head in a container containing the blood of his nobles so he could drink their blood, as it were. Tomyris did have a reason for what can be considered to be excessively brutal behaviour: Cyrus had treacherously killed her son after Tomyris had sent her son to see him. Christine is here illustrating the fact that the world can be a cruel place where women can be betrayed or victimized but that it is important for women to stand up for themselves and to turn, if necessary, the weapons of oppression back on the oppressors. But anyone with pacifist convictions or someone who entertains the idea that the New Jerusalem should contain only those who refrain from matters such as revenge and murder, may be surprised at the desire of Christine to place these women in the foundations of her City. On the other hand, as far as Christine is concerned, the City must be strong and protected and who is better able to symbolize that than the Amazons?

Another reason for focussing in on matters such as killing and warfare is that this realm is usually regarded as exclusively masculine as well as the most dramatic side of the public realm and its heroism. History is often thought to be the story of kingdoms, rulers, wars, conquests, and heroic deeds. By describing the Amazons as she does, Christine de Pizan removes female imagery away from the realm of the domestic and private by describing women who are more than equal to men in this particular area of the public realm.

An example of her desire to see women as able to compete with men in their field is Christine's account of the Amazonian queens Menalippe and Hippolyte. These queens, on hearing that Hercules and Theseus have invaded their land and that their soldiers are killing people in the night, ride out to meet the two men to take them on singlehandedly. They attack Hercules and Theseus personally and both manage to remove the enemy men from their horses. But Menalippe and Hippolyte are captured in the ensuing sword fight on the ground and are taken captive. Ancient sources, Christine de Pizan relates, try to explain Hercules' initial defeat by blaming his horse: what else can you blame when the most powerful man of Greece is defeated by a woman? Another aspect of Christine's descriptions of women is that they always remain feminine. Her descriptions of the physical appearance of her heroines is an indication of this. At one point, she describes the death of Queen Penthesileia of the Amazons on the battlefield. Pyrrhus, having ordered his men to have only one purpose in mind, that is, to capture Penthesileia during a battle, finally succeeds in having her surrounded. She is attacked and her helmet is hit off her head. Pyrrhus, before clefting her brain with his sword, sees her beautiful blonde hair flowing freely. In fact, all the Amazon women were, according to Christine's account, stunningly gorgeous.

Another characteristic which Christine attributes to the women she describes is that many of them are so proud and independent that they refuse all their lives to sleep with men, or, as in the case of the Amazons, only for the purpose of reproduction. Christine does not impose a binding view of marriage on her women: she praises the decision on the part of women to remain independent. This medieval view of the relationship between the genders is unique in western culture. In the times before and after this period, the ideal woman is married and oriented totally to the man or men who give her a purpose in life (we shall see, this view as especially prevalent in the 18th and 19th centuries). In the medieval view, in keeping with the teachings of St. Paul in the New Testament, marriage and relating to the other gender are not the highest ideals, but the highest ideals are spiritual, as Christine also argues. While in the Church the independence of women was partially taken away again by the fact that males were to rule over women, for Christine the ideal is it true independence: the capacity to cope for oneself in life.

The women Christine describes all through her book represent for her the best possible combination of male and female characteristics. She wishes to come to a reaffirmation of the feminine in two ways: on the one hand as not being any less than the masculine and able to compete with the masculine on its own ground; on the other hand as feminine, itself strong and beautiful.

4   Alternative Conceptions of the Historical

The second theme which I would like to discuss in light of Christine's book is that of the historical. Perhaps one of the most important questions here concerns the accuracy of the historical accounts and the implications of the accounts. At first sight, Christine does not seem to be overly conscientious about the historical authenticity of her sources, at least as measured by present-day standards.

An extreme example of this issue is Christine's account of Minerva.[5] Christine places her in the category of intellectual women, regarding her as a woman who invented a number of sciences. She expanded the

Greek alphabet so that more could be expressed and written in the Greek language, thus laying the foundation for the great tradition of Greek writing. She discovered numbers and a simple method of addition; the art of spinning wool and weaving; the making of oil by pressing olives and other fruits; the making of carts and wagons; making armour from iron and steel; the strategic ordering of men to form a fighting army; and making flutes, trumpets and other musical instruments. Our reaction to these claims today may be that they are completely out of order as historical facts. But Christine does have a very interesting argument to support her claims, an argument of demythologisation. Christine claims that the Greeks saw Minerva as a goddess precisely because of her wisdom and accomplishments. The Greeks could not believe that a woman was capable of such things and hence when she died they built a temple in Athens to her honour, calling her the goddess of wisdom, weapons and knighthood. In the temple, they placed a statue of her, that is, of the historical Minerva. Beside the statue they placed an owl to defend her, but also to symbolise the fact that both warriors and wise people must be alert day and night, whether against attack or in order to make the best of situations.

In this way, Christine not only demythologises the goddess Minerva in order to place a woman, Minerva, in the history books, but she also makes an interesting move here in terms of the theme of the New Jerusalem. For surely, in the same sense that it is daring to describe characteristics of God as being symbolised by Ladies and having ferocious Amazons in the city, it is also daring to have Greek goddesses living in this Judeo-Christian place. But for Christine de Pizan, if Minerva is not a goddess after all, but a highly talented historical figure, she fits into the city.

Another example of the issue of historical accuracy is Christine's inclusion of material from legends concerning the lives of the saints. In the last part of her book, she describes the life of St. Catherine of Alexandria. Perhaps it is no coincidence that the story of St. Catherine follows upon those of the Queen of Heaven, Mary, and of Mary Magdalene. St. Catherine receives this place of honour because she is, among others, the patron saint of philosophers. She was a philosopher who defended the truth of the Christian faith against heathen philosophers and she was martyred in this cause. Because her death was that of being racked on a wheel she is, somewhat macaberly, also the patron saint of wheel makers. The story of St. Catherine is as follows. She was the daughter of King Costus of Alexandria. One day, when she was eighteen, she was bothered by the bleating of sacrificial animals who were being gathered together for sacrifices to the gods by emperor Maxentius. She rushed to the temple where Maxentius was worshipping and proved to him by philosophical arguments that:

> ...there was only one God, Creator of all things, and He alone should be worshipped and no other. When the emperor heard this beautiful, noble, and authoritative maiden speak, he was completely amazed and utterly speechless; nevertheless, he stared at her intently. He summoned from everywhere the wisest philosophers known in the land of Egypt, then quite famous for philosophy, and some fifty philosophers were assembled who were quite unhappy to learn why they had been sent for, and said that a trifle had moved the emperor to assemble them from such distant lands in order to debate with a maiden. In short, when the day of the debate arrived, the blessed Catherine so successfully overwhelmed them with her arguments that they were confounded and unable to answer her questions. On this account the emperor was beside himself with anger, which had no effect at all, for they all converted, thanks to the divine grace in the holy words of the virgin, and confessed the name of Jesus Christ. The emperor had them burned for this disrespect, and the holy virgin comforted them in their martyrdom, assuring them that they would be received in eternal glory, and she prayed to God to uphold them in true faith. Thus, because of her, they were ranked among the blessed martyrs.[6]

After this event, Maxentius lusted after Christine, who repelled his advances. He had her imprisoned, tortured and starved her, but to no avail. He then had her placed on two wheels with razor edges turned against each other so that the person placed on the wheel would be cut in two. Catherine was placed naked on the wheel, the wheel was broken by angels and the torturers were killed. At that, the wife of the emperor was converted: he had her beheaded, along with other converts. Finally, Maxentius had Christine successfully beheaded. Although this story contains a great number of deaths, it is in Catherine and Christine's world view more important for a person to die in the faith than to live a godless life.

As to the question at issue here, that of historical accuracy, we may perhaps assume that both Christine and the medieval Church consi-dered stories of the lives of the saints to be historically accurate accounts. We can conclude that Christine was at least not creating a fanciful history merely for ideological purposes but was using a historical methodology acceptable in her time. On the basis of today's more stingent criteria for historical accuracy, the existence and dating of the life of St. Catherine is a problem. But I think that it is important to note that our present-day emphasis on historical accuracy has its limitations. By this I mean that modern people often fail to understand the importance of religious stories as inspiration: a matter vital for under-standing Christine de Pizan's project as a whole. In our abstract, rationalised culture abstract religious principles form the basis of spiri-tual life. We feel that we have no need anymore for illustrations, perhaps comparable to the example given in the introduction to this book, of Heidegger figuratively tearing the illustrations out of the Nietzsche text he is commenting on. Yet for medieval people, abstract principles were transmitted in concrete, inspirational stories such as that of St. Cathe-rine. The story points not so much to St. Catherine herself, but to the example of faith which she sets. The stories of the lives of the saints are to inspire people and ultimately to speak of the glory of God. In this sense, I think that it can be argued that the question of the historical accuracy of the stories of the lives of the saints is one which must be evaluated in light of the inspirational function of such stories in religious experience.

I think that there may well be a connection between the idea that the stories of the lives of the saints are inspirational and Christine's aim, discussed earlier, to describe the lives of noble, talented, wise and religious women in order to inspire her fellow-women and to improve their self-images as women. Nevertheless, historical accuracy and inspi-rational value are interdependent: an untrue historical fact is less inspi-ring than a true one. This problem has also presented modern feminists with methodological headaches, as I shall try to show in the next section.

5   Christine de Pizan and Modern Reconsiderations of History

Christine de Pizan and many women after her argue that the achievements of women in the public and intellectual realms have been under-reported in the history books. They argue that there were a great number of talented women in history who were ignored by male historians and culture. They then attempt to prove that women were and are capable of all the things men are, perhaps of even more, were they not ignored by history or prevented from being active in traditional male realms. Their opponents, on the other hand, would argue that there are perhaps only a handful of talented women in history and that this proves the natural inferiority of women in the public realm.

In the women's movement, this debate has moved in the direction of a critique of ideology. Women in the women's movement claim that it is not simply a question of historical material and facts but that there is a need for a re-evaluation of historical method itself. Perhaps history writing is something which serves the self-image of society and perhaps those who write history are the winners perpetuating their own victory. Perhaps, feminists suggest, there are also some faulty psychological dynamics going on when women are excluded or downgraded and when traditional patterns are continually repeated when writing history.

Those who wish to claim that there are a large number of great women in history who have been ignored by male historians and culture run the risk that their claims will be considered to be exaggerated. Those who claim that history has dealt fairly with talented women run the risk of being corrected by the research continually coming out. But perhaps the most insidious of those who enter into this debate are those who agree that women have indeed achieved great things in history but who use this fact to cover up the sexism in society. Praising the achievements of great women from the past can be a ploy to cover up the fact that these women struggled to an extraordinary extent to achieve what they did. In this sense, they are not typical of all women but their achievement is so rare because they were able to rise above the sexism in the societies in which they lived. Those who wish to call attention to great women may want to claim that there is appreciation in society for talented women and that therefore there is no sexism in society. In other cases, the examples of great women have been used against women: would you as a woman like to have a steely disposition or the same character as some famous role model? Such role models then get a negative connotation.

For Christine de Pizan, there were many great and talented women in history and they are a positive example of what women can do. Sexism for her loses all its justification if men would only consider what women are capable of. In this sense, Christine de Pizan is gloriously optimistic. But her views go further than sheer optimism: Christine de Pizan notes that it is important for people to think for themselves, to look beyond prejudices and received opinion. In this sense, Christine de Pizan stands half way between the medieval period and that of modernity, the time at which a new emphasis was placed on thinking for oneself and considering matters anew. In the next chapter, we shall see what the results of such rational methods are for the view of women and their role in society.

Notes

1   T. Ponfoort, "Inleiding" to Christine de Pizan, *Het Boek van de Stad der Vrouwen.* (Dutch translation, also by T. Ponfoort, of *Le livre de la Cité des Dames.*) Amsterdam, Nijgh en Van Ditmar, 1984, p. 7-17. For English language introductions, see: E.J. Richards, "Introduction" to Christine de Pizan, *The Book of the City of Ladies.* New York, Persea Books, p. xix-li. See also: C.C. Willard, *Christine de Pizan. Her Life and Works.* New York, Persea Books, 1984.

2   Revelation 21:9 – 22 :5.

3   Christine de Pizan, *The Book of the City of Ladies.* transl. by E.J. Richards. New York, Persea, 1982, p. 219.

4   Christine de Pizan, *The Book of the City of Ladies.* transl. by E.J. Richards. New York, Persea, 1982, p. 38-51.

5   Christine de Pizan, *The Book of the City of Ladies.* transl. by E.J. Richards. New York, Persea, 1982, p. 73-75.

6   Christine de Pizan, *The Book of the City of Ladies.* transl. by E.J. Richards. New York, Persea, 1982, p. 220.

6 Women, Reason and Science

1 Introduction

In the last two chapters, we considered the view of women presented by St. Thomas Aquinas in the scholastic tradition of the Middle Ages and the response to the medieval view of women by Christine de Pizan in terms of rewriting and re-evaluating this tradition. Modern philosophy is dated from the 16th century, the period when, in western thought, the break becomes definitive between the Middle Ages and modernity. This change is most specifically characterised by an orientation towards reason as opposed to the acceptance of the traditions of ancient Greek and medieval philosophy, of Christianity and the Church, as the basis for philosophy and philosophical method.

In this chapter, I would like to look at some implications of the new emphasis on reason for the view of women and their place in society. I will first look at the relevance for women of the new ideal of rational science in the modern sense of the word by discussing some of the ideas of Francis Bacon. Secondly, I will look at Descartes' idea of reason as providing universal access to knowledge for everyone. I will then turn to two issues raised by the views of Descartes: firstly, that of the relationship between the practical and the theoretical sides of reason and secondly, that of the abstract universality of reason. As we shall see, these two issues are relevant to the question of the view of women in the context of modernity.

2 Francis Bacon: Reason, Science and Women

Francis Bacon (1561-1626) is known as one of the founders of the "new science". In Bacon's view, the time has come to create a new scientific method, free of superstition. Because it would be entirely based on reasonable assumptions and logical steps of reasoning, it would be capable of freeing mankind from superstition as well. The task of science is to investigate nature and to discover its secrets in order to free mankind of all sorts of ills caused by nature, such as disease and natural disasters. Bacon sees nature as something good, but only insofar as its evil effects are brought under control by knowledge and the power of reason. The most famous statement which Bacon makes outlining the need for a new scientific method, as opposed to the methods of "the ancients" such as Plato and Aristotle and as opposed to the superstitious approaches to nature of the Alchemists, is found at the beginning of his book *The Masculine Birth of Time or The Great Instauration of the Dominion of Man over the Universe.*

The remarkable thing about the way in which Bacon presents his views here is his use of a number of male-female images and presuppositions. Bacon assumes that the scientist is male. He denotes nature as female, which is a traditional image for nature. His book opens with instructions to "my son" to put aside all prejudices and to aim for a more complete understanding of nature through science. He writes: "My intention is to impart to you, not the figments of my own brain, nor the shadows thrown by words, nor a mixture of religion and science, nor a few commonplace observations or notorious experiments tricked out to make a composition as fanciful as a stage play. No; I am come in very truth leading to you Nature with all her children to bind her to your service and make her your slave".[1]

The male scientist, according to Bacon, has the task of "wresting" the secrets of nature from her. In expressing this idea, Bacon uses terminology which is rather odd. Carolyn Merchant, in her book *The Death of Nature* discusses this idea of "wresting secrets" from nature, noting the parallel in imagery here used by Bacon with concepts more fitting to his other occupation, that of solicitor general and lord chancellor of the British government. In this role, Bacon was an advocate of torture (indeed, that is how he got promoted from the former government job to the latter by James I). He was active in the persecution of women for witchcraft and used the tactics of "wresting secrets" from them in the all-too-literal sense. In this context, Merchant finds terms such as "wracking" as used by Bacon disturbing.[2]

The second attitude which Bacon describes in sexual terms is that of the male scientist looking at nature with admiration, respect and an attitude of listening to what she says. Only the humble, devoted lover can expect nature to reveal her secrets. In this attitude, "The method must be mild and afford no occasion of error".[3] Bacon sees this courtship, as it were, ending in chaste and holy wedlock: "My dear, dear boy, what I purpose is to unite you with *things themselves* in a chaste, holy and legal wedlock; and from this association you will secure an increase beyond all the hopes and prayers of ordinary marriages, to whit, a blessed race of Heroes or Supermen who will overcome the immeasurable helplessness and poverty of the human race, which cause it more destruction than all giants, monsters, or tyrants, and will make you peaceful, happy, prosperous, and secure".[4] Bacon seems to assume that there are also "unclean" relationships possible between the scientist and nature, for example, those of sorcery and witchcraft. The chastity of matrimony symbolises the attitude which the scientist must take to nature, that of research and reason. The children, described in male terms as heroes and supermen who will prevail over the evils in the world, symbolise the power of reason and empirical knowledge.

The two attitudes, one of wracking secrets from nature, the other of modest courtship and holy matrimony, seem contradictory, but in fact are not. They express two possible ways in which a male can approach a female: by using power, control, and violence or submission, love, and gentleness. The ultimate aim is the same: to get something from her, in this case, to obtain truths from nature and control over her.

3   Theoretical Discussions and Implications

Although Bacon uses many other images and examples to illustrate his ideal of a new scientific method, his use of sexual imagery is significant. I think that a number of issues can be raised concerning this type of imagery and the presuppositions which underly it. These issues concern Bacon's notions of the masculinity of scientists and scientific thought as well as the ideals of control and manipulation of nature.

It is clear that for Bacon scientific activity is a male monopoly. This is no doubt due to the factual situation in his time: men were better educated than women, had more free time, associated with each other to increase scientific knowledge, and encouraged each other in these activities. Women kept to the home, were busy there, and did not participate in the public realm of intellectual pursuits. In the 16th century, it was considered unfeminine to participate in male activities such as doing science: such a woman was a "public" woman.[5] But, despite all the new emphasis on reason versus superstition, no change was considered in this situation by either Bacon or most other men, nor were changes made through some kind of intellectual revolution by women. As such, this is a curious fact, no doubt due to strong social and cultural influences.

Another issue which can be raised in light of Bacon's view of science is whether there is a specific kind of scientific thought and rationality which can be characterised as male thought.[6] What does it mean when Bacon addresses the scientist as "my son"? In other words, if scientific thought is done and is to be done exclusively by men operating within a certain intellectual tradition, will this give rise to an ideology of male thought? But what would that be? Feminist philosophers have noted that there are a number of possible characteristics of such thought: for example, the emphasis on abstraction and control which Bacon mentions as characteristics of his new science. This would mean that men want to fit the empirical, multifacetted elements of nature into theoretical frameworks and theories. The diffuse, the diverse, is categorised, systematised, and made "static". In a view such as that of Bacon, such characteristics seem essential to science and would, in his eyes, perhaps even necessitate the exclusion of female thought and values.

The feminist critique of the theoretical, abstract, and controlling nature of science and scientific thought is, of course, not uniquely feminist. Especially in the 20th century critique of western thought and the scientific mentality, the ideals of science as expounded by Bacon have been discussed at length. Feminists often see the root origin of the characteristics of modern science as the masculinity of this type of thought, created by men in a male mental atmosphere. Other thinkers have argued that various cultural influences are responsible for creating these characteristics of scientific and rational thought: for example, the influence of Christianity, through which nature came to be seen as abstractable and controllable because in this religion it has been demystified.

Feminists, again in keeping with similar attempts by other 20th century critics, have tried to formulate an alternative view of science. An example of the specifically feminist critique of this type of thought is presented by L. Irigaray in her concept of the "mechanics of fluids".[7] Irigaray argues that scientific thought, as male thought, has always been one-sided. She suggests that science should now begin to incorporate feminine elements, elements traditionally associated symbolically with the feminine and elements which reflect characteristics of the way women think. Irigaray argues that female thought is more fluid, focuses more on change, makes room for the chaotic and the irrational. It is unlike the strict, controlling, and static theory formation of male thought. She notes that a number of male thinkers have also reconsidered the characteristics of modern scientific thought. There have been many changes in modern scientific method that are a result of developments in relativity theory and quantum mechanics in which there is an acceptance of the limitations of theory, of the chaotic, the changeable, and the non-quantifiable. Sandra Harding, an American philosopher of science, even calls late 20th century scientific thought female thought because the move to postmodern conceptions in science is a move away from traditional norms of male thought.

It certainly seems true that in our culture there has been a move away from the ideals of control of nature and static theorising about nature. But some questions concerning the feminist critique do remain. I think that it can be argued that contemporary changes in the view of scientific method and the scientific attitude towards nature are emerging out of paradigm changes which have come about in science itself. And has contemporary science not been thought out mainly by men? In addition, the alternative view of nature as something we do not control or which should not be exploited in a ruthless fashion can also be seen as dictated by necessity, based on scientific testing of, for example, the environmental consequences of such exploitation, again done mainly by men. In addition, the lessening of the threat of nature and the environment to mankind makes control less necessary. For example, if one lived in an environment in which one could be eaten by a lion, one would want to control the lion population. In an environment in which lions are almost extinct or in which people are protected against attacks by lions, control of lions seems not only unnecessary but an attack on the right of lions to live and have their own territory. Perhaps such dynamics also account for the increased call to lessen our ideals of control of nature.

But even more troublesome are the questions concerning male and female thought. Are critics who now see the coming of the age of female thought in science not simply repeating the same preconceptions which have pervaded western thought in the first place? In other words, would not even Bacon himself agree that women are less rationalising and more attuned to nature than men? Perhaps we need to break through the sexism of seeing thought as male and female in order to avoid repetitions of stereotyping. It may not be wise to rehabilitate the old taboos concerning female thought as true after all, but now in a positive sense.

What would a new "female" "postmodern" science be like? A great deal of traditional science and the resulting technology is still valid thanks to the theoretical, abstracting and controlling characteristics of such thought. What, equally successful but without the negative side effects, could we replace it with? How radically could a new conception of science eliminate the negative side effects of the old science? If a new science is possible, how radically different would it be from traditional science? Is a new science only a change of icing on the cake of traditional science or is there a real possibility that in the future we may develop completely new paradigms? Or are the confusions now being caused by traditional science already indications of a paradigm change situation? Perhaps it is important, when asking these questions, to distinguish between theoretical science and technology, and between different fields in science, in which there are different theoretical fashions and developments. Sometimes in a certain science theories emerge which create a broader view of rationality or nature than was previously the case. Sometimes the development of theories have a direct, liberating impact for women. In that case, it is perhaps better for feminists to do science and keep a watchful eye on developments than to aim for a completely new type of female thought in science.

Another issue that arises concerns the effects on women of the kind of science for which Bacon argued. A number of thinkers have noted that male dominated science means that women are sometimes victimized by technology created by men. Very few women will want to hold that the practical, technological consequences of science have been all bad or have given them nothing at all. From switching on a light bulb to having medical treatment, everyone profits from the practical applications of science. The point, however, is that women have sometimes been treated instrumentally and unfairly by male dominated science. An example which is often cited is that of gynaecology. Historical developments in this field have been seen as controversial. For example, the development of tongs to deliver babies was an invention of a male doctor in the 18th century and led to people preferring doctors to midwives to deliver children. This was so despite the fact that the tongs were not in all cases good for the mother or child. Another area in which the interests of male doctors conflicts with those of the mother is the way mothers are made to deliver their children in positions more convenient for the doctor than for them. The greatest scandal in this field, however, was the epidemic of infections and deaths in the 19th century when women began to go in great numbers to hospitals to have their children. The result was that, in an age unfamiliar with bacteria and viruses, doctors without sterilized hands were the cause of innumerable deaths. In our day, controversy has arisen about the development of family planning medications made almost exclusively for female consumption. This issue takes on especially schocking forms in the third world where instances occur of women being given long lasting and strong anticonceptive medication which is not permitted in western countries. Another heritage of the battle between male and female interests in this field is the continuing strife between mostly male doctors and mostly female midwives. Although the midwives are making a comeback, for generations they have been depicted as dangerous amateurs.[8]

Bacon's view of nature as female lives on to this day, albeit in forms he himself did not anticipate. In the anti-science view of science, Bacon's ideas are perpetuated in the idea that women are closer to nature than men. On the other hand, it can be argued that because of that, they would never have allowed the world to become such an exploited, polluted and technologised place as it now is. But where would science and nature be if women had been in charge? We will of course never know, since science is one of the most strongly male dominated areas we have in our culture. Science done by women using different methods and having other values is therefore more part of the future than of the past.

4 René Descartes: Theoretical Versus Practical Reason

The second thinker whom I would like to discuss in this chapter is René Descartes (1596-1650). Descartes, like Bacon, emphasises the importance of reason in philosophy and science. He is known best for his famous statement of "modernity", found in the opening words of his *Meditations on First Philosophy*.[9] Descartes here states that he wishes, for the first time in his life, to free himself of all ideas which he has accepted as true on the basis of authority and tradition and to base his thought solely on the principles of reason. Hence his meditations: his aim, he states, is first, to eliminate everything which he has accepted hitherto as true, then to come to a rational, necessarily true foundation for all thought, and then to see the world anew in light of this foundation. Such a project is "modern" in the sense that it breaks with the notion that philosophy and science should be based on tradition, as it clearly was in medieval thought. Reason is now to become the final arbitrator of truth.

A considerable amount of research has shown that the view of Descartes as the philosopher of modernity and the forerunner of the Enlightenment of the 18th century is not entirely correct. Descartes had a Jesuit philosophical training, which was, however, considered innovative in his own time. Yet his philosophical background is still strongly influenced by concepts coming out of the scholastic tradition, apparent, for example, in his metaphysics and his attempts at formulating proofs of the existence of God. In this sense, Descartes is a symbol for the changes in western thought which were occurring in his time and in which he participated. Nevertheless, Descartes himself believed strongly in the ideal of reason. He notes that the entire inspiration for his philosophical and scientific thought is the idea of founding them on a unified system with mathematics at its basis.[10]

For women, Descartes' belief in doing away with ideas from the past not based on reason would seem to provide hope. Their natures and gender roles could be reconsidered in light of this new thinking, unencumbered by the weight of the traditions of the Greeks and the medievals. In fact, this was partially true: a number of women in Descartes' own time and afterwards did see his philosophy as a new inspiration and a statement of liberation.[11] This was primarily due to the "democratic" way Descartes saw knowledge. He speaks for example of *bon sens,* "good sense" and *sensus communis,* "common sense" or the natural capacity for arriving at true knowledge which all people have. All people of all classes and both genders can, according to Descartes, develop themselves intellectually in philosophy and the sciences. On this point, Descartes can be seen in the context of attempts by 17th century thinkers to broaden accessability to knowledge. An example of this is the widespread tendency, which Descartes also followed, to begin publishing works in the vernacular rather than in Latin.

Yet, as we all know, the true revolution in the belief in the intellectual abilities of women and the opening up of higher levels of education to women did not really begin to take place until the 19th century. In the following discussion of Descartes, I would like to look at some of the reasons for this lack of a breakthrough, linking these reasons to some of Descartes' own views and practices. The theme I have chosen to lead us through this discussion is that of the tension in Descartes' thinking between theoretical and practical reason.

5   The Practical Basis of Theoretical Thought

One of the most interesting aspects of Descartes' thinking about reason is his idea that theoretical reason, in order to develop, must do so under certain practical conditions. Since we can safely assume that one of the main barriers to women participating in science and academic pursuits is practical, it is all the more striking that Descartes actually discusses this issue with a woman, Princess Elisabeth of Bavaria.

During the 1640's, Descartes corresponded with Princess Elisabeth concerning philosophical, religious and personal matters.[12] Elisabeth was, of course, not an average woman of Descartes' time: she was a wealthy woman of a good family living in the elegance of the diplomatic center of The Netherlands, The Hague. For a woman in such a privileged position, it would seem that there is no real barrier for her to develop herself, to obtain a good education and to deepen her knowledge of philosophy and science. Yet her letters are full of complaints that she has no time to read and to think more deeply about the issues she is corresponding about with Descartes. A similar complaint was made by another friend of Descartes, Queen Christina of Sweden, who would get up at 5:00 a.m. in order to have some free time for reading and thinking. It would seem that the demands made on women in such high circles were considerable and that the notion of privacy and of free time to read and think were not very much part of the culture. This was most likely all the more a problem for women of the lower classes.

Descartes, in response to these complaints by Princess Elisabeth, notes that there are practical requirements for the exercise of reason and the development of theoretical thought. He notes that he himself has, in this respect, always followed a number of rules. The rules are related to the type of intellectual activity involved. In his letter of June 28, 1643 to Elisabeth, he writes:

> First, then, I note a great difference among these three kinds of notions, in that the soul conceives itself only by the pure understanding; body – that is to say, extension, figures, and movements – can likewise be recognised by the understanding alone, but very much better by the understanding aided by the imagination; and finally, the things that pertain to the union of the soul and the body are recognised only obscurely by the understanding alone or even by the understanding as aided by the imagination; yet they are known very clearly by the senses.[13]

Descartes here mentions three types of knowledge, corresponding to three mental funtions: that of pure intellect (e.g. metaphysics); that of intellect aided by the imagination (e.g. physics); and knowledge of the senses (e.g. everyday experience). The thinker must adjust his thinking habits to these distinctions. Descartes gives Elisabeth the following guidelines:

> ...I have never employed save very few hours each day at thoughts that occupy the imagination, and very few hours per year at those that occupy the understanding alone, and that I have devoted all the rest of my time to the respite of my senses and the repose of my mind; I even reckon among the exercises of the imagination all serious conversations, and everything that requires attention. That is what made me retire to the country.[14]

Descartes' time schedule no doubt reflects what for him is the best way of doing things and, considering his great achievements in philosophy and science, it obviously works. Yet the likelihood of Princess Elisabeth and a great number of other people following this type of schedule and coming up with any achievements at all is small. And not everyone can retire to the country for peace and quiet. Descartes, curiously, does not mention the fact here that there must surely have been a great deal of study behind his thinking: he was very knowledgeable about all the latest intellectual developments of his time. How – and when – is Princess Elisabeth to achieve anything like that? Of course, not many people in the world have achieved what Descartes has, but how is Elisabeth to achieve *anything* on the basis of this advice? Nor does Descartes mention the fact that the price he paid for his peace of mind was a solitary existence, having abandoned his lover and illegitimate daughter.

At issue here is "having no time". In the case of the privileged Princess Elisabeth, this may seem a trivial complaint. But what does it mean when women say that they "have no time" to achieve the same things as men in science or other academic pursuits? Perhaps having no time has deeper meanings: one is too tired, or one is not really interested, or one has taken on too many other marginal tasks which distract from what should be the main aim, or demands are made on a person which means that that person is robbed of the time for intellectual activities.

People tend to have time and make time for achieving things which are rewarding in a certain social-cultural setting. While for men there would be great rewards and admiration for intellectual achievements, someone like Princess Elisabeth may have been subconsciously influenced by the fact that her surroundings placed value on activities such as those of caring for her family and fulfilling her considerable social obligations. It is then admirable for both Princess Elisabeth and Queen Christina to have made the effort they did to "make time". For most women (and men), "time" is a reality which prevents them from achieving what they wish. A notable example of this is the fact that research has shown that in the years in which men obtain PhD's, women are having their children, a situation which creates a tremendous handicap for women who wish to pursue academic careers.

6   The Tension Between the Practical and the Theoretical

We saw in the discussion of Bacon's view of science as a male activity that it is possible to give "male" and "female" characteristics to thought and reason. The question concerning a possible difference between male and female thought also arises in the correspondence between Descartes and Princess Elisabeth. Perhaps it is a coincidence, but Elisabeth, the woman, advocates a concrete and practical position, while Descartes, the man, argues for a much more abstract and theoretical approach. The

issue which illustrates this difference in approach is that of the relationship between body and soul.

One of the main themes of the correspondence between Descartes
and Elisabeth is Descartes' dualism. In his *Meditations*, Descartes concluded that body and soul are manifestations of two distinct substances,
the material (body) and the mental (soul). These two substances, he
argues, have entirely different characteristics: body has extension, is
located in time and space, and hence is subject to the laws of physics.
Mind, he argues, has none of these qualities: it is immaterial, is not
locatable in any specific space and is not empirically observable. For
Descartes, the fact that body and mind have completely different
characteristics means that he has presented a proof of the immortality
of the soul. The only difficulty with his theory is the problem of the
interaction between body and soul. How can substances of an entirely
different nature interact with each other?

For Elisabeth, the metaphysical arguments used by Descartes to
prove his dualism do not fit in with her everyday experience of what it
is to be a concrete person. For her, mind and body are linked together
and influence each other. A human being is one interactive whole.

Descartes goes to great pains in order to convince Elisabeth that his
view is theoretically correct, even though he understands her intuitive
objections. Descartes also admits that in this particular case the truth of
metaphysics and the truth of everyday experience are difficult to unite;
instead, he argues that the results of knowledge obtained by the pure
intellect and by sense experience can be at variance with one another.
While our reason tells us that body and mind are totally different and
separate, our everyday experience is that of the unity of the two. In this
sense, his concession to Elisabeth is that she may think of the soul as a
kind of rarefied material and thus she can imagine the interaction
between body and soul. This is, however, only a method of imagining
the situation, not the metaphysical truth.

Gradually, the letters between Elisabeth and Descartes change in
tone and content. Elisabeth describes the tensions she is experiencing
caused by family matters and her illnesses as a result of these problems.
It emerges that she is subject to psychosomatic ailments, such as
depression and lack of energy. Descartes responds very openly and
sympathetically, offering her comfort and advice. From this correspondence, one can see that Elisabeth was very concretely concerned with

the relationship between body and soul, experiencing their interrelationship in her own life.[15]

In the end, it does seem as though Elisabeth, together with other critics of Descartes' dualism, had some influence on him. His last published book was *The Passions of the Soul*, containing a physiology of human functioning and emotions.[16] With its more empirical approach, this book attempts to deal with the issues raised by Elisabeth. Descartes posits the idea that the rational soul lives in the pineal gland, surrounded by the cavities of the brain. Animal spirits move throughout the body, ending up in these cavities and by their movement they give information to the soul. Thus Descartes tries to explain the influencing and being influenced of the body by the soul, thus accounting for their interaction. Descartes did not feel comfortable with the book, not publishing it immediately after it had been written. This book lacked, no doubt, the rigor and search for necessarily true metaphysical truths which his earlier work on the body and soul had had.

Were Elisabeth's objections to Descartes' dualism typically female ones? Could the debate between Elisabeth and Descartes demonstrate that male and female thought are based on different intuitive insights? Would Descartes' separation of body and soul have had no influence at all if his intellectual peers had been women instead of men? Would not the whole biological make-up of a woman protest at the likelihood of a soul independent of the body?

Unfortunately, these hypotheses have never been tested by a poll on how men and women react to Descartes' views (although that would be a very interesting experiment indeed). Many male philosophers were also troubled by Descartes' dualism and philosophers such as Malebranche, Spinoza, Berkeley, La Mettrie, Kant and Husserl struggled to find different answers to the puzzles surrounding dualism with which Descartes had presented them. Many contemporary philosophers would also object to a strong dualism of body and mind, although, interestingly enough, there are still a considerable number of Cartesian theories around in present day philosophy of mind. The dualistic theories tend to be in areas in which forms of physicalism or information processing theories play a role. Philosophers who are more oriented to a view of people in organic or wholistic terms are usually less dualistic.

What, then, influences a theory and its acceptance or rejection in areas such as science and philosophy? Is gender a factor, together with cultural and intellectual-historical presuppositins and developments? But the question which continually arises when speaking about the issue of the relationship between gender and thought is whether women really want their thinking to be seen as more concrete, earthly and practical than that of men? Would that mean a new ghetto for "female thought" or something positive, a different voice in a male dominated discussion?

As was noted earlier, there are examples of prominent female thinkers who took the ideas of Descartes concerning the equal ability of all people to reason as their inspiration and the justification for their intellectual activities. Descartes' friendships with Princess Elisabeth and Queen Christina also show his inspirational and sympathetic qualities. Yet these women were relatively privileged and Descartes made no effort to engineer social change on a broader scale. Descartes was anything but a social activist by nature or a practical philosopher concerned with social questions.

Descartes of course had no notion of an alternative type of female thinking: his idea of reason is based on the ideal of mathematics, an area in which answers are either right or wrong, independently of the thinker. His concept of reason means on the one hand equal access, on the other hand that women had to function within the parameters of a view of science and philosophy based on concepts developed by men.

7   Conclusions

In this chapter, a number of issues concerning reason, science, and women have been raised. More questions remain after mulling over the discussion of these issues than have been answered. Perhaps answers are not even desirable, considering the misuse that can be made of them on both sides of the gender gap. Can science be called "male", nature "female"? Is there such a thing as male and female thought? How are we to explain the fact that the achievements of males and females in areas such as science and philosophy are so different? Why did the birth of the new ideals of reason and science not create new opportunities for the education and development of women? Why were the social and gender-political conventions not changed in light of the new fashion in thinking? Who had the responsibility for making such changes: people such as Bacon and Descartes or revolutionary women themselves? Or are the changes hoped for by some women at that time doomed to failure because society was not at all prepared for them?

This period did not, as we have seen, become the start of a revolutionary historical liberation of women. This is not only because of the failure in the 17th century to bring about such change in society as a whole, but because the Enlightenment of the 18th century did not build on the positive insights which arose in the 17th century. We have seen that Descartes' view of the universal access to knowledge for everyone and reason as something all people have potentially has positive implications for the liberation of women. It would seem that the Enlightenment, in holding reason and human equality to be its highest values would bring ideas such as those of Descartes into practise. Unfortunately, however, in terms of a view of society and the nature of women and their roles in it, some very different developments came about. In the next chapter, I will describe how they come to expression in the philosophies of Rousseau and Kant, and how Mary Wollstonecraft attempted to show that such philosophies did not apply Enlightenment ideals of reason to women.

Notes

1   Francis Bacon, *The Masculine Birth of Time or The Great Instauration of the Dominion of Man over the Universe*, in: Benjamin Farrington, *Francis Bacon: Philosopher of Industrial Science*. New York, Schumann, 1949, p. 62. This passage is also quoted by C. Merchant, *The Death of Nature*. New York, Harper and Row, 1980, p. 170. See also, F. Bacon, *Works*. Collected and edited by J. Spedding, R.L. Ellis, and D.D. Heath. Stuttgart, Fromann, 1961-1963.

2   C. Merchant, *The Death of Nature*. New York, Harper and Row, 1980, p. 168-169.

3   F. Bacon, *The Masculine Birth of Time or The Great Instauration of the Dominion of Man over the Universe*. in: Benjamin Farrington, *Francis Bacon: Philosopher of Industrial Science*. New York, Schumann, 1949, p. 62.

4   F. Bacon, *The Masculine Birth of Time or The Great Instauration of the Dominion of Man over the Universe*. in: Benjamin Farrington, *Francis Bacon: Philosopher of Industrial Science*. New York, Schumann, 1949, p. 72.

5   See for example, Angeline Goreau, "Alphra Behn: A Scandal to Modesty", in: D. Spender ed. *Feminist Theorists. Three Centuries of Key Women Thinkers*. New York/Toronto, Random House, 1983, p. 8-27.

6   See for example, Sandra Harding, "Is Gender a Variable in Conceptions of Rationality? A Survey of Issues", in: *Dialectica* 36 (1982, 2/3), p. 225-242. This article also contains a large number of further references to literature on this issue, p. 240-242.

7   L.Irigaray, *Ce sexe qui n'en est pas un.* Paris, Minuit, 1977. English translation: *This Sex Which Is Not One.* transl. by C. Porter with C. Burke. Ithaca, New York, Cornell University Press, 1985, p. 106-118.

8   For a detailed discussion concerning this particular issue, see: Adrienne Rich, *Of Woman Born.* New York, W.W. Norton, 1976. See especially Chapter 6, "Hands of Flesh and Blood, Hands of Iron".

9   R. Descartes, *The Philosophical Works of Descartes.* transl. by E.S. Haldane and G.R.T. Ross. Cambridge, Cambridge University Press. Volume 1, 1973, p. 144-149.

10 Bernard Williams, "Descartes, René", in: P. Edwards, ed. *The Encyclopedia of Philosophy.* New York/London, MacMillan and the Free Press/Collier MacMillan, 1967. Vol. 11, p. 344.

11 For example, Madame Marie de Gournay who, inspired by Descartes' view of rationality wrote, among other books, *L'Égalité des hommes et des femmes.* See: Janna Thompson, "Women and the High Priests of Reason", *Radical Philosophy* 34 (1983, Summer), p. 10. There were a considerable number of well-educated and talented women in the 17th century who wrote on philosophy, among them Anne Conway and Anna Maria van Schurman. In addition, a point of debate found in 17th century European literature is the discussion as to the natural inferiority, superiority or equality of women to men. An example of this type of literature is Johan van Beverwijck's book *Van de wtnementheyt des vrouwelicken geslachts,* (On the excellence of the female gender) published in 1639 in The Netherlands.

12 See J.Blom, *Descartes. His Moral Philosophy and Psychology.* Sussex, Harvester Press, 1978, for this correspondence.

13 R. Descartes, *Descartes – His Moral Philosophy and Psychology.* transl. by J.J. Blom. Sussex, Harvester Press, 1978, p. 113.

14 R. Descartes, *Descartes – His Moral Philosophy and Psychology.* transl. by J.J. Blom. Sussex, Harvester Press, 1978, p. 114.

15 R. Descartes, *Descartes – His Moral Philosophy and Psychology.* transl. by J.J. Blom. Sussex, Harvester Press, 1978, p. 118-241.

16 R. Descartes, *The Philosophical Works of Descartes.* transl. by E.S. Haldane and G.R.T. Ross. Cambridge, Cambridge University Press, Volume 1, 1973, p. 329-427.

7 Rousseau, Kant and Wollstonecraft. The Education of Women

1 Introduction

In the previous chapter, we considered the relationship between the development of ideals of reason and the "new science" and the view of the nature and roles of women. Although few breakthroughs occurred for women in the 16th and 17th centuries, one would expect that the 18th century, the time of the Enlightenment, would finally see the start of liberating developments. This is, however, not the case for a number of reasons. Although the philosophical-theoretical view of the Enlightenment is that it is a period of strongly developed rationality in thought, in society the emphasis was on art and artifice. In the growing middle and upper classes of Europe, in the fine urban cultural settings of which Paris seems to have been the epitome, the search for elegance and refinement implied that, among others, gender roles were more strongly defined than ever and that a complex code of "morals and manners" was developed to guide relationships between the sexes.[1]

The literature of this period on morals and manners is based on the idea that there is a male and female nature as well as an ideal dynamic between men and women which reflects their natural and social tendencies. The purpose of this type of literature is to formalise the male-female relationship, thus creating principles by which a young man or woman can be guided towards his or her appropriate characteristics, habits and talents by means of a social and sexual education. The concept of "education" as used here is different from the contemporary idea of education since it is both broader and narrower. On the one hand, it is narrower because it does not pass on scientific and cultural knowledge in the many subjects as we know them today. On the other hand, this concept of education can be seen as broader in the sense that it includes guidance for the way to behave, virtues to have, ideals to strive for and social skills to be developed, all of which enable a person to fit into a social and sexual role.

In the views of education we will be looking at, males and females are thought to need a different education to suit their masculinity and femininity, their rationality and lack of it. The development of human reason in its "neutral" connotation is only applicable to men. In this literature, men are regarded as rational and as having the task of thinking deeply and critically, thus freeing themselves from tradition: the Enlightenment ideal. Women, however, in contrast to Descartes' ideas on this matter, are not to share in this training. In some cases, as we shall see, women are referred back to authority and tradition as that which is to regulate their thought and behaviour.

In this chapter, I will discuss some views on the education of women by looking at two writings in the genre of morals and manners: Jean-Jacques Rousseau's *Emile* and Immanuel Kant's *Observations on the Feeling of the Beautiful and the Sublime*.

Rousseau and Kant both take the idea of human nature as their point of departure. They ask what the relationship is between human nature in general and the nature of men and women. The way they answer this question has implications for their views of the education of men and women and the roles they are to play in society. After my discussion of these issues in Rousseau and Kant, I will turn to the British philosopher Mary Wollstonecraft's critique of Rousseau's views on these issues. I will then discuss some issues related to the way she presents her alternatives for the education of women.

2 Human Nature, Male and Female Nature

For Rousseau (1712-1778), the basis for a theoretical view of people is the concept of nature and human nature. In contrast to the Christian tradition, as expressed by St. Thomas Aquinas, human beings, according to Rousseau, have not received their nature through divine creation. Instead, mankind evolved from a state of nature towards life in civil society. For this reason, the point of departure for speaking about human nature is in terms of primitive man and his and her evolution. The state of nature is for Rousseau the situation in which our most fundamental characteristics were formed and which still represents the most authentic expression of who we really are as human beings. Culture is for Rousseau a later, possibly deforming, development. Therefore, in order to determine the basic natures of men and women, Rousseau goes back to an analysis of their natures and gender roles in primitive society.

According to Rousseau, men and women at first lived fairly independently of each other, meeting only for the purpose of reproduction. When the female conceived, she drove away the male and raised the children on her own. In Rousseau's view, men and women only begin to be dependent on each other with the development of social structures. With the emergence of the idea of the home and a community based on an economic structure, people discovered that a certain role division was useful: the man protecting the home and his children, hunting and providing, the woman taking care of the home and the children. Basic to Rousseau's ideas concerning the differences between male and female is that males are physically stronger than females and yet are dependent on them for sexual gratification; and that females should use all their powers and charms to gain control over men, thus compensating for their lack of physical strength. A woman must develop characteristics which make her attractive to men, able to bind a man to her; in order to do this, she has to give up her independence and learn to exploit the male weakness for sexual gratification. A man must develop characteristics of being strong, independent, rational and in control; on the other hand, he too has become dependent on the woman. The result of this division of strengths and weaknesses between the genders is that it enables them to manipulate each other to get their way.[2]

In his book on education, *Emile* (1762), written at the request of a female friend, Rousseau develops a theory of education which he believes reflects the natural tendencies of male and female.[3] Education, a product of civilisation which can pervert the natural tendencies of mankind, must be employed, perhaps paradoxically, to bring out the best of the natural. Education must therefore be in harmony with nature and help nature come to its full potential in culture. In Book V of *Emile*, Rousseau discusses general principles for the education of women and gives his impression of "the perfect woman", Sophie, whom Rousseau himself, the mentor of Emile, has selected to be Emile's wife.[4]

In Rousseau's view, if there are differences between men and women, this must be reflected in the type of education they are to have. He opens this book with the question of the extent to which men and women share a common human nature and to what extent they differ from each other. Rousseau admits that he does not know how far the differences extend between male and female: do they pertain only to their body build or also to their character? Rousseau resolves this vital issue with the rather casual remark that men and women are mostly equal and similar, but the perfect man does not resemble the perfect woman. Women must develop their strengths and advantages, mentioned above, in the battle of the sexes.

An important aspect of this sexual strategy for women is that she learn to (appear to?) please the male. She is to exploit all her feminine charms. She must take care to have the best possible outward appearance, must learn to show off her delicacy and weaknesses, and, perhaps most importantly, she should demonstrate at all times her reticence in desiring a man: modesty is a strong weapon in the battle of the sexes. She must thus play a game with the man, being attractive to him and at the same time not giving any indication of the strength of her feelings. A man must be kept guessing, at a distance. His strong urges will then inflame him with passion; this passion is fuelled by his urge to protect his own self-love and pride. In this way, the woman, according to Rousseau, physically weaker and more in need of a man than he is of her, will be able to tie him to her.

The educational process through which these feminine skills are developed is described at length by Rousseau. Rousseau, for example, states that girls, like boys, are, when young, equally aggressive, enjoy playing outside, and love exercise. But young girls soon show their true nature and impulses when they begin preferring to play with dolls and show their love for mirrors, jewelry, and lovely cloth. In having these interests, they show that their nature is to develop their taste and that they want to be considered to be attractive.[5] Rousseau also notes that little girls dislike learning to read and write, but can fantasise for hours about becoming just as attractive as their dolls when they grow older. Since their own attractiveness is their major asset, educators should encourage this type of play.[6]

A girl should also be taught to accept the authority of her elders. This is an important issue for Rousseau since this will prepare the girl to later accept the authority of her husband. Her educators can encourage this by, for example, helping a girl dress her doll tastefully and to make matching combinations of clothes and accessories. Noting that the little girl needs help with this, Rousseau sees this activity as a first step in learning that she is dependent on others. Boys are more independent and therefore should be given rational reasons for doing or not doing certain things, but girls are to be simply told on authority what to do.

Another way to teach girls to accept authority is to keep them busy at tasks in the home, confining them all day to the house. Rousseau realises that this form of feminine education in the home and the concomitant confinement may mean that women become physically less strong than men who as boys are allowed to have noisy fun and are allowed to play and exercise more. Rousseau does not resolve this issue entirely. On the one hand, he expresses admiration for strong women, noting the achievements of the women of Sparta who, he says, exercised naked in public; on the other hand, he would not like to apply such a model of physical education on a refined French woman, arguing that a certain amount of fragility and dependence are essential characteristics of the attractive woman. As in many other cases, he tries to justify his view with the concept of nature, stating that women "naturally", especially after puberty, have less of a tendency to want strenuous physical exercise than men.

In addition, an important part of the education of girls is developing their social skills. Women, according to Rousseau, are social creatures, they are more accepting of others, they desire to be of service to others, more so than men. Women are more polite, being better than men at pleasing others with compliments. For Rousseau, these tendencies also have a natural and sexual basis. Women are much less polite and charming to other women than to men, and show affection to other women only in public when men are present, in order to make the men desire the same affection for themselves.

As to religion, a girl should not, as in the case of a boy, be encouraged to form her own opinions, but to follow those of her parents and in later life those of her husband. This is, according to Rousseau, because a woman is unable to reason deeply enough to come to her own conclusions in this area. Men have the task of questioning and judging religion in the light of reason: women must therefore leave this decision to their husbands. Moreover, this is, according to Rousseau, the best way to promote harmony in the home because it prevents conflicts arising about religion and principles. For Rousseau, religion has a social dimension in the sense that it represents social conformity. Rousseau therefore argues that women, in their religious training, should be taught that God is watching them continually, thereby keeping them on the straight and narrow path. Hence women should be taught general piety rather than religious principles.[7]

3   The Ideal Woman, Sophie.

Beyond formulating general guidelines for the education of women, in this book Rousseau describes the ideal wife for Emile, Sophie. Sophie is the daughter of decent, down-on-their-luck gentry living in the country: her mother was of a good family but was disowned by them, her father had money but lost it. She is their only daughter, 15 years old when she meets Emile, but in all respects she has mastered the art of being a woman. She knows how to dress simply but seductively (men, Rousseau says, want to take off her simple but artful clothes in their imagination). She has natural talents for singing and moving well. She enjoys doing women's work, such as sewing and lacemaking, and she has, from an early age onward, helped her mother run the household. She does not disdain to take over tasks from servants when they are unable to perform them. She has an obsession with cleanliness, hating above all things that are dirty. She had a fondness for eating when young (bonbons) but has now overcome that, although she does eat feminine things: dairy products, sugared things, pastry and sweets and only rarely meat. She does not drink alcohol and eats in moderation. Her mind is not brilliant, but she is a good judge of character. She is lively but at the same time she has learned to control this, although she will always have an element of sensitivity and caprice. But she never knowingly does wrong things and when she does, she will cry and regret it: she is an obedient, devoted and loving daughter to her parents. She has a simple idea of religion, seeing virtue as all-important. Because of her honest and direct disposition, she has a dislike for empty conversations and superficial compliments, as well as the vices of society people. She has a very mature ability to see through artifice. Because she is an energetic no-nonsense person, she does not feign exaggerated weakness such as putting her arm on that of an older man when going from one room to another. As far as her formal education is concerned, she has read only one book in her life, a work by François Barrême on how to keep household accounts.

Her parents decide that because of her maturity she is ready to get married. Her father tells her that her marriage will not be arranged but that she will be able to choose her own husband. This is in keeping with Rousseau's principle of a natural upbringing which takes into account the preferences of children. Sophie is sent to the city to live with an aunt in order to be introduced to society. Because of her anti-superficial and virtuous nature she does not find the men she meets attractive and returns to her parents' home in the countryside. This too is in keeping with Rousseau's philosophical ideas: the city is corrupt, the country pure. At this point, her life begins to show the first signs of crisis. To her embarassment, feelings of sexual desire and male-female love start to manifest themselves. Her mother finally gets her to confess that she is confused because she has fallen in love with the main character of the second book she has read in her life, *Telemachus* by Fénelon. At this point, she is ready to fall in love with a real man and marry. The real-life manifestation of the romantic ideal of Telemachus is of course Emile. Like Sophie's father who lets her make her own choices, Rousseau feels that Emile too must make his own decision about his choice of a wife. With this difference, however, that Rousseau has already selected Sophie and is arranging matters behind the scenes. Rousseau takes Emile away from the city into the country to meet Sophie at the home of her parents, the perfect setting. No stain of city life must enter this scene. Once more, the country setting reflects the purity and virtue of Sophie and Emile.[8]

Both geographically and inwardly, Sophie is naturally good, beautiful and pure. This is an important fact for understanding the type of education which Sophie receives. Rousseau does not believe that she needs much formal education. The characteristics of Sophie which make her such a suitable bride for Emile have been nourished by wise and loving parents who have given her the ability to master the important "musts" for being an eligible mate: an attractive outward appearance, a knack for household management, and a suitable disposition. It is only after her marriage to Emile that she will receive a more formal education, for (and this is of course the irony of it all) otherwise Sophie would be too boring a mate for the well-educated Emile. But what is very important is that Sophie may never become a threat. Never must there be a moment in which Emile is not, by virtue of his gender and education, in control. Repeatedly, Rousseau calls the husband of a woman, including Sophie's Emile, her master.

To demonstrate the problem of knowledge as power and the sexual taboos surrounding education, I will quote perhaps the most shocking passage in which Rousseau speaks of this issue. Rousseau begins by stating that an educated man must not marry a totally uneducated woman, but on the other hand, if he has no choice, an uneducated woman is preferable to the other extreme:

> But I would still like a simple and coarsely raised girl a hundred times better than a learned and brilliant one who would establish in my house a tribunal of literature over which she would preside. A brilliant wife is a plague to her husband, her children, her friends, her valets, everyone. From the sublime elevation of her fair genius she disdains all her woman's duties and always begins by making herself into a man after the fashion of Mademoiselle Enclos. Outside her home she is always ridiculous and very justly criticized; this is the inevitable result as soon as one leaves one's station and is not fit for the station one wants to adopt. All these women of great talent never impress anyone but fools. It is always known who the artist or the friend is who holds the pen or the brush when they work. It is known who the discreet man of letters is who secretly dictates their oracles to them. All this charlatanry is unworthy of a decent woman. Even if she had some true talents, her pretensions would debase them. Her dignity consists in being ignored. Her glory is her husband's esteem. Her pleasures are in the happiness of her family.[9]

Perhaps we could, in a spirit of generosity, grant Rousseau the point that many women are made happy by successfully marrying, performing their domestic duties and being surrounded by a loving family. On the other hand, Rousseau does not seem to be very generous in his appreciation of the achievements of women such as Mlle Enclos (who is mentioned more often, always with horror, in this book).

After Emile and Sophie have fallen in love, they begin courting. Their courtship, described at length by Rousseau, reflects Rousseau's view that a relationship between a man and a woman is based on the strength of a woman's modesty and the driving force of a man's desire for her. Sophie, extremely noble and modest, is only gradually won over by Emile. Emile's emotions and desire for her are, however, so strong that he suffers and persists. During their courtship, Sophie's education is continued by means of the long conversations the lovers have:

> It is both a touching and a laughable spectacle to see Emile eager to teach Sophie all he knows, without considering whether what he wants to teach her is to her taste or is suitable for her. He tells her about everything, he explains everything to her with a puerile eagerness. He believes he has only to speak and she will understand on the spot. He fancies beforehand the pleasure he will have in reasoning and philosophizing with her. He regards as useless all the attainments he cannot display to her eyes. He almost blushes at knowing something she does not know.
>
> Therefore, he gives her lessons in philosophy, mathematics, history – in a word, in everything. Sophie lends herself with pleasure to his zeal and tries to profit from it.[10]

Sophie's abilities to learn about these subjects from Emile is limited. As Rousseau comments:

> The art of thinking is not foreign to women, but they ought only to skim the sciences of reasoning. Sophie gets a conception of everything and does not remember very much. Her greatest progress is in ethics and in matters of taste. As for physics, she remembers only some idea of its general laws and of the cosmic system.[11]

Most likely Sophie's cursory understanding of what Emile is telling her is not due to her feminine nature, as Rousseau would like us to believe, but because Sophie is being expected to understand what Emile has learned in the course of a long time of studying in the span of lover's conversations (Emile prefers talking to her while he is on his knees in front of her). This seems to be a striking example of the double standard which men apply to themselves and to women in order to affirm their own intellectual "superiority". As to Sophie's preference for ethics and esthetics, this is a point taken up, as we shall see later, by Kant.

The main purpose of the fifth chapter of *Emile* is to describe the courtship and marriage of Emile to a woman who is right for him. The context of the description of Sophie's education is, as Wollstonecraft points out, sexual. The book ends with the announcement by Emile that his young wife Sophie is pregnant with his child.

I will now turn to a most curious document inspired by the reading of Rousseau's *Emile*, Kant's *Observations on the Feeling of the Beautiful and the Sublime*.

4   Kant's *Observations on the Feeling of the Beautiful and the Sublime*

Rousseau's *Emile* was published in 1762, Kant's *Observations* in 1764. The two works are connected not only in time, but there is even a philosophical legend about the relationship between the two books. Kant (1724-1804) was known at Königsberg for living a very regular life. Every afternoon he would take a walk at precisely the same time: so precise was he that the townspeople said that one could set the clock by his schedule. Kant is said to have missed his walk only once: when he was reading Rousseau's *Emile*. Unfortunately, this delightful story is most likely untrue, but it does indicate the extent to which Kant's *Observations* are influenced by Rousseau's views.[12]

The book consists of four chapters in which Kant describes various aspects of culture and society in terms of the concepts of the beautiful and the sublime. The third chapter deals with the idea of the beautiful and the sublime with respect to male and female.

Like Rousseau, Kant opens this chapter with a discussion on human nature. He states that men and women are all human beings and thus share a common nature. Nevertheless, Kant states that the humanity male and female have in common may not obscure the fact that the male and female are very different as well. This idea, also expressed by Rousseau, can be seen as the classical philosophical approach to male and female nature: they share a common humanity, based on a shared rationality and emotional world, but underlying this sameness are differences.

Kant claims that the rationality of male and female can be distinguished in terms of female-beautiful and male-sublime. Female rationality is directed to the amiable, the pretty, and the concrete. Male rationality is directed to that which is deep, theoretical, general, and abstract. The female is, in her daily life, concerned with the aesthetic and judges everything on the basis of what is or is not pleasing. For the female, her appearance, her house, and her friends should all have a pleasing character. The male is less concerned about such charms: he is more involved with "duty" and the heavier things in life.

Like Rousseau, Kant sees the natural tendencies of the two genders as emerging in childhood. Kant states that girls tend to love being pretty and attractive, they like pure things, are sensitive to things improper, love being busy with trivial things, are casual and like laughter, comport themselves well in company, are kind to others, prefer the beautiful to the practical, love jewelry, are sensitive to insults, have a good intuition about people, and should ultimately aim to make men more gentle and refined.

Kant also deals with the question of female virtues and morals. Female virtue is described as being beautiful, male virtue as sublime. Women have, according to Kant, moral sentiment. They avoid evil not because it is evil, but for the aesthetic reason that it is reprehensible. A woman will not act according to certain virtues because she is ordered to do so, but because she feels that it is attractive to do so. Women were not created to follow principles, according to Kant, although he adds that it is also exceptional for men to follow principles. Women are blessed with a good heart, a willingness to do good, and a feeling of what is proper and fitting.

Kant also mentions a number of feminine "weaknesses", stating that they are ultimately "beautiful faults": a woman's sensitivity, her aversion to insults, her vanity which makes her want to appear beautiful, appealing and charming, her humour and changes of mood – all these can be attractive. For all that, Kant feels that women should restrain themselves: too much vanity, for example, will turn into a real fault.

As to sexuality, women have, according to Kant, a natural aversion to unchastity: their purity is what they value most and their greatest fear is to be called unchaste. Women have a highly developed feeling of shame and an aversion to male sexual banter. Modesty in a woman is described by Kant as "a form of noble simplicity and naïveté connected to an outstanding character".[13]

The description given by Kant of male and female characteristics is one that is based on the notion of complementarity: the two genders enrich each other's lives and modify each other's character. The noble, deep-thinking man has his complement in the sensitive and intuitive woman; the male orientation to ethical principles is modified by the female's good-heartedness and spontaneity; female delicacy and modesty refine overly strong male tendencies towards crudity and improper desires.

Kant modifies his idea of the complementarity of the two genders somewhat by stating that while the male is noble and the female beautiful, both genders have elements in them of the other. Through male-female contact and mutual influence, people are made more complete, thus avoiding the development of one-sided gender characteristics or extremes.

For Kant, the complementarity of the two genders means that neither male nor female need feel insulted at the way he describes them: after all, he says, what he is describing are the natural differences they have and the ideals towards which they rightly strive. A criticism which is often made of the so-called complementarity thesis is precisely that it tends to cover up the fact that negative judgments are being made. This comes to light when comparing the characteristics attributed to men and women. A great number of women might well feel that they have not been justly described, having gotten short shrift in the division of characteristics.

Finally, this essay is written explicitly by Kant from his own male point of view, referring to "we men" as opposed to "women". This is not only stylistically the case, in that the first person is male and the third person female, but it also emerges in the language used to describe the two genders. Women are described as being "attractive" and "charming", terms which refer to the impact of women on men. Indeed, Kant argues that this impact of women on men is what it is all about, even for women themselves: their greatest concern is men. Terms used to describe men are more external and neutral: they stand on their own, not in relationship to someone else and men are described as being oriented to things other than women. One can see this, for example, in Kant's description of the sublime and principled minds of men. Women direct themselves to men, men to higher things. At certain points, however, Kant does refer to male feelings about themselves and how they appear to others, as, for example, when he refers to the fact that men have a fear of appearing to be ridiculous.

Although this essay is not an explicitly pedagogical one, as was Rousseau's *Emile*, Kant does give some guidelines for the education of women. According to Kant, the education of women must be suited to the rationality of women and to the way women operate. Women do things easily, unlike men, who need deep thought and intense labour to accomplish something. A woman, Kant says, who attempts to perform deep mental activity deserves only cool admiration because she is then sacrificing all that is beautiful in her. Mentioning the examples of Madame Dacier and the Marquesse de Chastelet, he states that all they need to complement their intellectual achievements is a beard.[14] Women, he states, will never be successful at academic activities in fields such as geometry, philosophy, physics, history, or geography. They should, however, be taught something in these areas in order to be able to understand social chit chat and general conversations about them and in order to (strangely enough) understand them in terms of what can be learned from them about women. This latter aim is not a feminist one, however: what a woman can learn about herself from such an education are interesting stories and perhaps a moral lesson or two.

In summary, Kant's view of the education of women resembles that of Rousseau in a number of respects. Like Rousseau, he bases his view of education on the idea that it must serve to bring out natural male and female characteristics and he sees the fulfillment of the development of the beautiful characteristics of the female as being marriage and keeping house. It is the woman who brings the aesthetics, warmth and charm to the home. Kant also gives examples of the horrors of women with a formal education who follow intellectual pursuits: he replaces Rousseau's Mlle Enclos with his own examples of Madame Dacier and Madame du Châtelet.

Both Rousseau and Kant attempt to find a firm basis for their theories in human nature. Yet many people today would consider their ideas to be quite contra-intuitive. Perhaps this is a warning that an appeal to nature is not at all self-evident. One can even go further and say that theories of male and female nature will always be suspect because they tend to cover up the influence of culture on the interpretation of nature.

5 Mary Wollstonecraft. Reason versus Passion

Mary Wollstonecraft (1759-1797) is one of the most important forerunners of the women's movement of the 19th century. She had only a short life, but it was one of commitment to women's rights, inspired by her intellectual background and her own considerable abilities. For Wollstonecraft, women have a right to an education equal to that of men. A contemporary of Rousseau and Kant, Mary Wollstonecraft travelled to France after the beginning of the French revolution in order to observe its progress and results at first hand. She was by then already acquainted with the work of Rousseau and wrote, in 1792, an attack on his theories of education for women as expressed in *Emile*.[15]

In the literature, Wollstonecraft's attack on Rousseau is aptly termed an attack of reason versus passion.[16] Wollstonecraft accuses Rousseau of tainting the Enlightenment ideals of reason and equality with what she calls the demands of male passion. Her own cause, she argues, is that of reason: a no-nonsense, non-sexist view of the education of women. In a sense, however, Wollstonecraft herself is passionate in her passion for reason to prevail and in her outrage at Rousseau's pinning women down to the sexual images, needs and desires of men.

Wollstonecraft's main concern in her critique of Rousseau are the sexual and sexist overtones in his description of Sophie's education.[17] She quotes Rousseau's views and then comments on them. Her first point is that Rousseau wishes a woman to be educated according to her female "nature" and in such a manner that she will be attractive to men. Wollstonecraft argues that the ideal woman, according to Rousseau, is attractive, weak, frivolous and is to be educated in a way which leads to "a system of cunning and lasciviousness". Women are to learn to play a sexual game with men. Physical and mental weakness is encouraged to make them seem vulnerable. But this weakness has a twist: it is to be employed to gain control of men, or at least to capture their sexual interest. Wollstonecraft argues that the aim of education for women should not be formulated in terms of male desires or in terms of "an education of the body". They should be educated in a manner which is best for them as people. Women, Wollstonecraft notes, are not really being educated in Rousseau's guidelines for their education. Wollstonecraft argues that women have a lot more to cope with in their lives than satisfying men. Noting that even Rousseau states that male-female love only lasts a short time, she says that there is no justification for limiting the education of women to a sexual strategy which will only help a woman through the first decades of her life. For Wollstonecraft, the development of reason is the most important thing for people because it enables them to cope with their feelings and the vicissitudes of life. Rousseau, she argues, ultimately gives advice which leads to women becoming sickly and unable to cope, especially after they have lost everything they depended on: their youth and attractiveness.

Wollstonecraft states that her alternatives for the education of women may lead to the sacrifice of the attractiveness of these women to prejudiced men such as Rousseau. We saw in the consideration of Rousseau's concept of education in *Emile* that education is to further and not to diminish the possibilities of women on the marriage market. Wollstonecraft, in response to this idea of Rousseau therefore ends her discussion of Rousseau's concept of education with the words:

> ...I earnestly wish...that Fortune, slipping off her bondage, will smile on a well-educated female, and bring in her hand an Emilius or a Telemachus...There have been many women in the world who, instead of being supported by the reason and virtue of their fathers and brothers, have strengthened their own minds by struggling with their vices and follies; yet have never met with a hero, in the shape of a husband.[18]

Wollstonecraft hopes, however, that such prejudices can be overcome and even if they are not, women are not to be overly concerned with this problem. A good education and independence, an ability to cope with life, means a strong and healthy relationship with a man is possible.

Strangely enough, Rousseau and Wollstonecraft in fact agree that the goal of the education of a woman is to create someone who is strong, healthy, dependable, attractive, wise, mature, rational, and able to cope with life and other people. Yet, Wollstonecraft, as we have seen, claims that the type of woman who is formed by Rousseau's education is someone who is weak, dependent, manipulating, irrational and ignorant. Wollstonecraft and Rousseau differ about the way in which they think education functions to create a healthy person capable of forming positive relationships. Rousseau lays a strong emphasis on the fact that, to start with, a woman must have a "naturally" good disposition which accords with the natural tendencies of the female gender. It is only on the basis of her natural capacities that she can be nurtured to develop characteristics such as that of good judgment and maturity. For Wollstonecraft, an education which includes more formal, abstact content is essential not only for the development of a man's mind, as Rousseau thought, but also for a woman's mind. This is, I think, the essence of Wollstonecraft's critique of Rousseau's "education of the body".

6 Conclusions

In my concluding remarks, I would like to return to two aspects of Wollstonecraft's response to Rousseau: firstly, her critique of the role of a "sexual code" in education and secondly the function of repetition in Wollstonecraft's critique of Rousseau.

In Wollstonecraft's response to Rousseau, a major theme seems to me her attack on the sexual code inherent in his view of the education of Sophie. In the Enlightenment, we are confronted with the development on the one hand of very strong ideals of reason, education, and the making of one's own decisions in all areas of life; on the other hand, there seems to be a renewed and strengthened affirmation of a traditional sexual code in which a taboo is placed on a formal, rational, education for women as well as on the public display of a woman's intellectual achievements. There is no doubt as to the effectiveness of such a code, a code by which, as Wollstonecraft notes, women are blackmailed. If one does not follow the code, the result is no husband and a bad reputation. Proof of the force with which the sexual code worked is the fact that in one 19th century dictionary, the name of Mary Wollstonecraft was listed as synonymous for the word "prostitute".[19] Her heroic character and tragic life cannot, however, be summed up with this term. The reason for such an outrageous association is that certain intellectual pursuits were identified with the "public" realm, a realm in which women, properly identified with the "private" realm, should not participate. If they did, they were "public" women, a term also associated with loose women. Two examples of such public intellectual activity are the publishing of books (even innocent books of poetry) and the running of a salon or publically having intellectuals as friends. While Wollstonecraft was courageous enough to publish her books, there is also a long tradition of women writing books and either publishing them under a pseudonym, making small private editions, or not publishing them at all in order to avoid such social taboos.[20] Wollstonecraft also lived in the other part of the "public" intellectual realm, openly having intellectuals as friends on an equal basis with herself. Ironically, Rousseau of course himself participated, albeit against his will and impelled by financial necessity, in the salons of Paris, often run by women.[21]

The interesting part of this is that the taboos applied to women at the time of the Enlightenment went together with an increase in the number of well-educated women. It is, I think, almost impossible to analyse clearly the dynamics taking place in the historical sense (a problem we will see return in the next chapter on the 19th century). Did the male desire for a very "feminine" image have anything to do with the growth of the number of women capable of intellectual pursuits? In which social classes was the contrast between an "intellectual" and a "feminine" woman an important one? And, on a deeper level, did the emphasis on women-in-the-home, being weak and superficial have anything to do with male fears of what would happen if women were to reject such roles and images? Are we dealing with merely superficial fashions which prescribe what it is to be an attractive woman or are the views of Rousseau historically deeply embedded in French culture (a claim Wollstonecraft at one point makes)?

Wollstonecraft's reaction to Rousseau is primarily on the level of sexual dynamics. Her struggle with Rousseau concerns his concept of femininity. On a personal level, it is no wonder that Rousseau's ideas raised such outrage in Wollstonecraft. There is an implicit promise, which Wollstonecraft also mentions in her critique of Rousseau, that if women are the way he thinks they should be that they will be able to fascinate men and bind them to themselves. Men, Rousseau promises, will fall lock, stock and barrel for a woman educated along the lines of his philosophy. Of course, most women, like Wollstonecraft herself, want a man but at the same time definitely do not see in themselves the characteristics which Rousseau says should be "natural" to them. Wollstonecraft herself suffered severely in this respect. Abandoned by her lover, she at one point attempted suicide by jumping off a bridge into the Thames in London.[22] Hence the (unintentional) cruelty of Rousseau's arguments for Wollstonecraft.

The essence of the matter here, it seems to me, is that, as Wollstonecraft says, the notion of "education" has become confused. Education is used by Rousseau in the double sense of learning, developing rationality, judgment and knowledge (primarily for men), and on the other hand in the sense of learning the sexual game of life (primarily for women).

The second aspect of Wollstonecraft's response to Rousseau which I would like to say something about is a stylistic feature of her reaction, which I shall call "repetition". Of course, Rousseau's own views on women are repetitious. Even though cultural settings change, there are many elements in his view of women which have been repeated by men throughout history. But Wollstonecraft, in her chapter on Rousseau, herself repeats, extensively and literally, the (for her) preposterous and negative things which he says about women. This is a characteristic of much of the writing done in the women's movement: a critique is presented in which the criticised ideas are repeated and then rejected.

Mary Wollstonecraft justifies this technique of repetition as a way of confronting Rousseau with the error of his ways. Another reason she gives for using this technique is that she is doing it so that people will believe that she is stating Rousseau's position correctly. But the phenomenon of repetition is, I think, more complicated than that.

Repetition can enforce ideas or it can serve to criticise and ironise ideas unacceptable to an author. But why give currency to unacceptable ideas by repeating them? It seems to me that it is not the strong who repeat the negative things said about them and done to them, but the weak. The strong rewrite history to show their glory and strength, the weak rewrite history to show the insults and exclusion. Often such writing from out of the standpoint of exclusion can produce anger and bring about change. But it is also painful to repeat ideas that one finds unacceptable. But over and over again, women are confronted with this dilemma. For Wollstonecraft, the process of reproducing painful ideas is the struggle for a new world, for the vindication (the beautiful term she herself uses) of the rights of women. And, as we have seen in this chapter, one of these rights is the very important one of access to a universal education, equal for men and women. Therefore, even though it is painful to repeat ideas one finds reprehensible, it can have some effect. The right of women to an academic education began to be realised in the 19th century with some important developments, the movement for universal public education for boys and girls and the start of the admission of women to universities.

Notes

1   Wollstonecraft uses the illuminating expression "morals and manners" to describe the literature on the relationship between the sexes in her time. See: M. Wollstonecraft's "Introduction", to: *A Vindication of the Rights of Woman*, London, Dent, 1929/1977.

2   R.F. Beerling, *Het cultuurprotest van Jean-Jacques Rousseau. Studies over het thema pathos en nostalgie*. Deventer, van Lochum Slaterus, 1977, p. 129-135; J.B. Elshtain, *Public Man, Private Woman*. Princeton, Princeton University Press, 1981, p. 148-170; J. Flax, "The Patriarchal Unconscious", in: S. Harding and M. Hintikka, eds., *Discovering Reality*. Dordrecht, Reidel, 1983, p. 264-269.

3   J.-J. Rousseau, *Emile*. transl. by Allan Bloom. New York, Basic Books, 1979 and London, Penguin, 1991. In Book XI of the *Confessions*, Rousseau describes the publication and reception of *Emile*. See: J.-J. Rousseau, *Confessions*. Baltimore, Penguin, 1967.

4   J.-J. Rousseau, *Emile*. transl. by Allan Bloom. London, Penguin, 1991, p. 357-480.

5   J.-J. Rousseau, *Emile*. transl. by Allen Bloom. London, Penguin, 1991, p. 365-366.

6   J.-J. Rousseau, *Emile*. transl. by Allen Bloom. London, Penguin, 1991, p. 367-370.

7   J.-J. Rousseau, *Emile*. transl. by Allen Bloom. London, Penguin, 1991, p. 376-378. It is interesting to note that the Pythagoreans, about 2,000 years earlier, also saw the function of religion for women in terms of developing their virtues and piety.

8   J.-J. Rousseau, *Emile*. transl. by Allen Bloom. London, Penguin, 1991, p. 393-410.

9   J.-J. Rousseau, *Emile*. transl. by Allen Bloom. London, Penguin, 1991, p. 409. Rousseau's claim that behind the achievements of an educated woman stands a male ghost-intellectual resembles the intriguing insinuations of Socrates that Aspasia's speeches were ghost-written.

10 J.-J. Rousseau, *Emile*. transl. by Allen Bloom. London, Penguin, 1991, p. 425.

11 J.-J. Rousseau, *Emile*. transl. by Allan Bloom. London, Penguin, 1991, p. 426.

12 I. Kant, *Opmerkingen over het gevoel van het schone en verheven*. Dutch transl. by H.P. Blok of Kant's *Beobachtungen über das Gefühl des Schönen und Erhabenen. (Observations on the Feeling of the Beautiful and the Sublime.)* Sneek, van Druten, 1919, p. 142.

13 I. Kant, *Beobachtungen über das Gefühl des Schönen und Erhabenen*, in: W. Weischedel ed., *I. Kant Werke*. Darmstadt, Wissenschaftliche Buchgesellschaft, 1960. Vol. 1, *Vorkritische Schriften bis 1768*, p. 858.

14 I. Kant, *Beobachtungen über das Gefühl des Schönen und Erhabenen*, in: W. Weischedel ed., *I. Kant Werke*. Darmstadt, Wissenschaftliche Buchgesellschaft, 1960. Vol. 1, *Vorkritische Schriften bis 1768*, p. 852. Madame du Châtelet was known especially for her research and book about Newton's physics. A fascinating biography of Madame du Châtelet is: N. Mitford, *Voltaire in Love*. Penguin, 1957.

15 For biographical information on Wollstonecraft, an excellent source is: M. Wollstone-
craft, *The Collected Letters of Mary Wollstonecraft.* ed. by Ralph M. Wardle.
Ithaca/London, Cornell University Press, 1979. See also: "Introduction" by Ralph M.
Wardle, p. 27-50.

16 M. Gatens, "Rousseau and Wollstonecraft: Nature versus Reason", *Australasian
Journal of Philosophy, Supplement to vol. 64,* June 1986, p. 1-15, and M. Brody, "Mary
Wollstonecraft: Sexuality and Women's Rights" (1759-1797)", in Dale Spender, *Femi-
nist Theorists. Three Centuries of Key Women Thinkers.* (New York/Toronto, Random
House, 1983), p. 40-59.

17 M. Wollstonecraft, *A Vindication of the Rights of Woman.* London, Dent, 1929/1977.
(First published in 1792). Chapter v, p. 86-102.

18 M. Wollstonecraft, *A Vindication of the Rights of Woman.* London, Dent, 1929/1977,
p. 102. That Wollstonecraft's complaint is not out of date was recently proven. Recent
research has shown that well- educated, professional women in their 30's and 40's are
the least successful of their generation on the marriage and relationship market.

19 M.A. Warren, ed. *The Nature of Woman.* Inverness, California, Edgepress, 1980,
p. 498.

20 Angeline Goreau, "Aphra Behn: A Scandal to Modesty", in: Dale Spender, ed. *Feminist
Theorists. Three Centuries of Key Women Thinkers.* New York/Toronto, Random
House, 1983, p. 16.

21 J.-J. Rousseau, *Confessions.* Baltimore, Penguin Books, 1967, Book VIII.

22 R.M. Wardle, "Introduction" to *The Collected Letters of Mary Wollstonecraft.* I-
thaca/London, Cornell University Press, 1979, p. 45-46.

8   Schopenhauer and Nietzsche versus the Suffragists. The "Natural" versus the "Unnatural"

1   Introduction

In the previous chapter, some 18th century ideas about the role of education and artifice in regulating relationships between the sexes were discussed. The 19th century in Northern Europe is a "heavier" century in the sense that great emphasis was placed on maintaining the values of the middle class citizen, or, to put it in English terms, on Victorianism and the maintainance of class structures. Looking back on this century, it is clear that it was a century on the verge of a new world order whose social structures were to be changed drastically by the First World War. It was also a century which, while maintaining traditional values, saw some of the greatest intellectual innovations in history and created strong impulses for the revolutions that were to follow: we need only think of the enormous impact of scientific discoveries made in the 19th century and the revolutionary nature of ideas such as those of Freud, Darwin, Marx and Nietzsche. It is therefore not surprising that in this century a tension arises between those who wish to maintain traditional values with respect to women and the family while at the same time revolutions, among which the feminist movement, were taking place.

The women's movement of the 19th century was a variegated movement, with differing backgrounds and influences forming it. Historically, the development of the movement can be linked to the effect of the French Revolution (as Wollstonecraft had already done at the time of that revolution). Women had seen that revolution pass without the promises of freedom, equality and "brotherhood" being extended to them. Although there was, in the first stages of the French Revolution, a concern for women's rights and their freedom to participate in the democratic process, this soon dissipated. In fact, the French Revolution, like so many other revolutions, attempted to alter existent structures, but the actual work of change, as in the case of universal suffrage for males, took much of the 19th century to accomplish. In this respect, it can be argued that the Suffragist movement of the 19th century was part of a broader social movement coming from the desire to implement the ideals of the French Revolution. But drawing such a historical line gives the Suffragist movement a legitimacy which its critics at the time were not prepared to give it: the movement was seen as a scandal which violated the propriety of ethical and social conventions or as simply a silly phenomenon.

There were, however, some very good reasons for the issues raised by the women's movement. At stake were matters such as the right to vote, to inherit and hold property and measures to prevent the dependency, impoverishment and exploitation of women left without a male to take care of them. Because there were political and social issues such as these at stake, not all the women who supported the women's movement were radicals simply wishing to overthrow the established order. A large number of women from religious and socially active backgrounds were concerned, for humanitarian reasons, with the plight of women.[1]

In this chapter, I will try to show the way in which Schopenhauer and Nietzsche reacted to ideas on the liberation of women. In the first part of this chapter, I will argue that despite their reputations as critics of their society and time they were nevertheless quite reactionary defenders of the middle class. Their tactic was also a traditional one: attributing certain natural characteristics to male and female as a justification for existent social roles. They saw traditional patterns as "natural", innovation as "unnatural". One of the strongest arguments they used to criticise change and the women's movement was to say that ideas were being launched which go against true female nature, male-female relationships and existing images of men and women. In the second part of the chapter, I will focus on the discussion of whether Nietzsche's perspectivism and his view of "the woman as truth" is as liberating as has been argued by some critics. Does this concept contribute to women's liberation or does it reflect Nietzsche's sexism?

2   Schopenhauer "On Women"

Arthur Schopenhauer (1788-1860) is famous for, among other things, his personal misogynism and his notorious essay "On Women". This essay is generally considered to be the most negative text on women in the history of philosophy. In light of some of the other texts discussed in this book, it is clear that this is not the case. Rather, Schopenhauer's text can be considered to be a good summary of some of the "traditional" views held by a number of the philosophers discussed in this book. Perhaps its tone is sharper, more reactionary than the texts of earlier periods. This is, as I noted earlier, most likely due to the fact that in the 19th century the tug of war between the genders began on a larger scale in the context of social change.

It is not entirely clear from Schopenhauer's text whom exactly he is describing when he is describing "women". It can, I think, be argued that Schopenhauer does not have one woman or one kind of woman in mind, but, most likely unconsciously, he describes various manifestations of the feminine: the child, the mother, the middle class wife, and the prostitute. What these typologies have in common is that they are chosen from out of the male perspective: the perspective of what a woman can mean for a man. Schopenhauer's style in this respect resembles that of Kant and Rousseau. His discourse concerns "we men" and "those women". Despite the use of the "we" versus "them" style, he claims that his descriptions are generally or super-genderly valid.

Schopenhauer opens his essay with a claim that the greatest value of women lies in "mothering". He states that women are primarily made for reproduction and nurturing. Men need to be cared for by women: that is why caring is their greatest virtue. As to their other characteristics, Schopenhauer notes many features of women in a rather incidental fashion. To summarize some points in his considerable list of female characteristics: women are not intended for great mental or physical exertion; they contribute to life by suffering; a woman's life is trivial; women are childlike; young girls have been given exceptional qualities of attractiveness in order to attract men; older women no longer need this attractiveness and hence are unattractive; women have weak powers of reasoning; their intuition is good; they spend the money men earn; women are pragmatic and prosaic; women are kinder to others but less principled to others than men are; women lack a sense of justice; women are cunning; women lie more easily than men; women are by nature enemies because they all have "the same profession"; their difference in "rank" is dependent on the achievements of their men and is thus more precarious and less differentiated than the differences among men; women are not attractive as such but the male sexual drive makes them seem attractive; women do not have a purely objective interest in things, their only interest is to dominate men; women have never achieved anything great in culture; they are the inferior sex in every respect; women should not be indulged or honoured: the oriental way of treating women is preferable to western gallantry; women do not have a right to equal rights with men because they are inferior to men; men are by nature polygamous, so marriage is a sacrifice for men; prostitution is a reflection of the natural tendency of men towards polygamy and is caused by the prohibition on having more than one wife; polygamy would mean more subordination of women, a good thing, since that would put an end to the phenomenon of the "European lady", the type of woman who wishes to "have" a husband, a position in life, wants him to be monogamous, wants chivalry and equal rights.[2]

Are these merely personal impressions on the part of a philosopher who, despite having had a large number of affairs, never got along with a woman until he was around 70 years old? There are a number of anecdotes about Schopenhauer which illustrate his difficult relationship to women, notably about his fights with his mother and his landlady. Friedrich Nietzsche, commenting on Schopenhauer's difficulties with women, states that Schopenhauer's misogyny is not an isolated personality quirk. He sees it as part of the deepest dynamic from out of which Schopenhauer lived, all part of his tendency towards nihilism, pessimism and asceticism. Moreover, Nietzsche claims that Schopenhauer needed enemies to function: these enemies are sexuality, sensuality, women, Hegel, and even existence itself.[3] Nietzsche is, of course, not a particularly objective judge of personality, but this analysis is an indication that even among his contemporaries Schopenhauer was seen as having a rather odd attitude towards women and life.

But surely Schopenhauer's essay "On Woman" would not have become as famous as it did if it were merely the reflection of personal, eccentric opinions. Surely there must be some truth to the essay, it must touch some kind of chord in people in order for it still to be read – and for it to continue to raise blood pressures.

Is it possible to show that there is some kind of "logic" in Schopenhauer's seemingly incoherent summing up of female characteristics? I think that a number of points can be mentioned which reflect patterns in Schopenhauer's observations about women which are based on social reality. Firstly, a major factor which seems to underlie Schopenhauer's characterisations of women is their lack of access to education. This would explain his claim that women are less rational, less capable of great achievements in cultural and academic areas, that they are "down to earth" in their views of situations and in the decisions they make, that they are less capable of "objectivity" than men, that they are childlike in many ways. All these characteristics, it seems to me, are developed through education. Secondly, many of the characteristics Schopenhauer mentions are due to the lack of opportunity for women in society. His arguments that women seek to attract men, that they obtain social status through men, that they are manipulative and cunning, that women are rivals, all point to characteristics of people who are socially powerless and dependent. Lastly, a number of the observations which Schopenhauer makes seem to reflect male frustrations with social codes concerning male-female conduct and relationships. His view of women as unattractive, his resentment of monogamy, his dislike of showing respect for women, his acceptance of prostitution as the fulfilling of normal male needs, all point to sexual-social frustrations.

From this analysis, it would seem that all of Schopenhauer's points of criticism of women could be resolved if he were to support the liberation of women. If women were to obtain a good formal education, have the opportunity to hold jobs and if there were a liberalisation of the mores of marriage, he would surely be pleased at the improvement. Schopenhauer, however, argues that because of their natural inferiority, women do not have the right to equal rights with men. Schopenhauer's idea of the natural inferiority of women is based on his conviction that their power of reason is less than that of men and on the presupposition that the characteristics of women which he has summed are natural and hence unchangeable. For this reason, there is no way out of the impasse in which Schopenhauer places himself and women: women's liberation could help to take away their perceived faults and weaknesses, but these same faults and weaknesses are used to justify not liberating women.

Schopenhauer uses another peculiar argument to oppose the liberation of women. This is his assertion that women may not claim more rights from men besides the great concession they have already received, monogamy. Men have sacrificed enough for women, in his view. Obviously, both arguments form barriers against the liberation of women and are used to leave the power of men as well as of society unchallenged.

3   Nietzsche and Middle Class Society

The German philosopher Friedrich Nietzsche (1844-1900) greatly ad-mired the work of Schopenhauer in his early days. Nietzsche, as I indicated earlier, was later to reject what he considered to be the nihilism, asceticism and pessimism in Schopenhauer's philosophy of the will. But Nietzsche did have in common with Schopenhauer a tradi-tional view of female characteristics and a suspicion and rejection of the women's movement of his time.

Nietzsche's views on women are perhaps best described as a combi-nation of theory and personal experience.[4] He lost his father and younger brother by the age of five and grew up in a family consisting solely of women: his mother, his sister Elisabeth, his father's mother and two unmarried aunts. This situation at home meant for him submersion in a female, 19th century middle class environment with a strong Lutheran religious atmosphere. I think that it is possible to interpret Nietzsche's views on women in light of this middle class background as well as in the context of his views of society and social change in general. Nietzsche, like Schopenhauer, bases his views on women on what are claimed to be natural and unnatural characteristics.

In one of the most famous passages which Nietzsche wrote on women, the discourse "Of Old and Young Women" in his book *Thus Spoke Zarathustra*, Nietzsche describes what he sees as both the top layer and the underlying dynamics in male-female relationships.[5] This passage seems to me almost a parody of the middle class perspective, including its tensions. As in the case of Schopenhauer's essay on woman, Nietzsche's summing up of female characteristics is haphazard. Just as in the Schopenhauer passage, it is possible to fill in a background of social practices and personal preferences underlying the descriptions.

In this passage, the perspective on women is an explicitly male one, seeing the woman as oriented totally to the man, family and domestic concerns. The description of the nature of women is extremely heavy-handed. According to Nietzsche, women are basically oriented to their husbands and children. That is why matters such as attracting a male, pregnancy, and raising children are their main concerns. The nature of women is directed to the realm of the natural and biological: in a sexual sense, women serve as "recreation" for men, they are playthings; in an emotional sense, love is their fiercest emotion and honour: a woman's hate is directed towards the man who does not want to have her, her feelings of fulfillment consist in doing what a man wants. As was also the case in Schopenhauer's description, women are seen as less educated, rational and honourable than men. Nietzsche states that women are bitter, base, and irredeemably shallow. Although Nietzsche claims to have a very different view of women than Schopenhauer, this passage from *Thus Spoke Zarathustra* shows how pervasive the impact is of the social situation in which these philosophers found themselves: the stifling atmosphere of women tied down to biological and domestic concerns, with men feeling both threatened and claiming natural superiority over them.

4   Speaking about Women

One sees in both Schopenhauer and Niezsche an unease in speaking about women. The philosopher must first overcome a barrier of taboo or embarassment in revealing his preferences or prejudices. This is perhaps the reason why Nietzsche places the passage on old and young women within a framework. The comments made at the beginning and the end of the passage raise a number of questions of interpretation. The passage begins as follows:

> Today as I was going my way alone, at the hour when the sun sets, a little old woman encountered me and spoke thus to my soul:
> "Zarathustra has spoken much to us women, too, but he has never spoken to us about woman".
> And I answered her: "One should speak about women only to men".
> "Speak to me too of woman", she said; "I am old enough soon to forget it".

Zarathustra is asked to speak of women to an old woman. When he protests that men should only speak about women to other men, the old woman replies that it is a good thing that she is old enough to forget what is being said. As such, this comment concerning age is interesting: already in ancient Greek society a distinction was made concerning the social-sexual status of young and old women. Old women were more free in their movements and in what they could do, say and think than young women. This is no doubt connected to the idea that young women are part of the sexual dynamic and the reproductive process, and that hence the taboos and rules governing their behaviour are to be applied in a strict fashion. Older women, less attractive and no longer of reproductive age, are considered to be less subject to sexual codes. An old woman may therefore hear this description from Zarathustra but a young woman may not. Could it be that his description of a young woman's nature and behaviour would give her a certain amount of awareness of herself, of men and how they see her? Would that influence her behaviour and her own sexual-social desires so that she might even want to break out of the traditional patterns? Whatever the answers to those questions, there is something smug and superior about the description which Zarathustra gives of young women. The context in which Nietzsche places his remarks on old and young women points to the fact that his aim is not liberation but rather maintaining the social order in which men determine who women are.

The end of the passage is as follows:

The little old woman answered me: "Zarathustra has said many nice things, especially for those who are young enough for them.

"It is strange, Zarathustra knows little of women and yet he is right about them! Is it because with women nothing is impossible?

"And now accept as thanks a little truth! I am certainly old enough for it!

"Wrap it up and stop its mouth: otherwise it will cry too loudly, this little truth!"

"Give your little truth, woman" I said. And thus spoke the little old woman:

"Are you visiting woman? Do not forget your whip!".[6]

Here the old woman seems says that what Zarathustra has said is in fact suitable for being heard by a young woman. She herself then as it were offers Zarathustra a truth in return – a truth which is even "older", that is, more suitable for mature people, than the truths which Zarathustra presented. This truth, the old woman says, must be kept secret: "Wrap it up and stop its mouth: otherwise it will cry too loudly, this little truth!". This truth is that when visiting a woman, one should take a whip.

The atmosphere of complicity between Zarathustra and the old woman which expresses the the power of speaking about gender relationships at this point moves forward into a deeper dimension: we have here an expression of the feelings of power and powerlessness which can occur between the two genders. There is a strange incident in Nietzsche's life to which this remark can be linked. In the period when writing *Thus spoke Zarathustra,* Nietzsche was in love with Lou Salomé, and, at the end of their relationship, on a trip through Switzerland, Nietzsche urged her and their friend Paul Rée to have their photograph taken at a professional photographer's in Basel. In 19th century style, the photographer had a number of background scenes and props in front of which his customers could pose. Nietzsche chose the scene of a rural cart, with Lou in the cart and he and Paul Rée as horses before the cart, with...Lou wielding the whip.[7] The three participants in this photo session were later profoundly embarrassed by this act, yet it says something very strange about the comment of taking a whip when seeing a woman. Apparently Nietzsche felt powerless against Lou Salomé; hence the fantasy of turning the situation around, a fantasy in which the male is in control.

It seems to me that there is something very unhealthy about both Nietzsche's and Schopenhauer's attitude towards women. Perhaps for both of them the power of women, especially that of female sexuality, is frightening. As was argued earlier, the stifling atmosphere of 19th century social-sexual norms makes the situation all the more difficult to get out of. Perhaps the attraction of Nietzsche to Lou Salomé rested on the fact that she was a liberated woman, a person who wanted to have a good education and wishing to have a "non-traditional" marriage. In this sense, Nietzsche may have (unconsciously) realised what I have already argued with respect to Schopenhauer: that even though he argues for a solution to the tensions in the relationship between men and women in terms of the repression of women, the real solution may actually be found in the liberation of women.

Finally, a curious aspect of this passage is the old woman's comment that even though Zarathustra seems to know little about women, he tells the truth about them. The old woman asks, ironically perhaps: is this because with women all things are possible? One can interpret this question as suggesting that anything one says about women will to some extent be true. It is of course a truism that statements about people are to some extent multi-interpretable: take the example of horoscopes in the daily newspaper which speak of characteristics and events in the lives of any person at all, applying only a few categories. But for Nietzsche this multi-intepretability of the feminine has another meaning as well. Nietzsche means that woman is changeable, she is not as solid and set in her character as a man. This idea of the indeterminacy of the feminine comes back elsewhere in Nietzsche's work when he speaks of women and the feminine.[8] This theme is also already referred to implicitly in the passage from *Thus spoke Zarathustra*, in which *men* are described as childlike and playing. If Nietzsche sees the feminine as the symbol of truth does this mean that Nietzsche has a high regard for women after all? On this reading, can the feminine even be considered to be the future of western thought?

5   Woman as Truth

Nietzsche regards the classic philosophical idea of truth as a typically male idea. It is a male misunderstanding that through earnest searching it is possible to find the one truth about the one reality. Women are capable of seeing through this illusion because of their attitude towards life and the way in which they experience themselves. Nietzsche agrees with the "feminine" idea of truth in that he believes that there are many truths about many aspects of reality. He calls this the perspectival view of truth. While the pre-Socratic philosophers and the post-Socratic Diogenes realised that truth and reality were changeable, the Socratic and Platonic tradition gave western philosophy its guiding idea that there is one reality, one truth, and one rationality and that it is the task of the philosopher to think according to these standards. Plato, Nietzsche argues, wants to "fixate" truth in an Idea. An Idea is some-thing which is static, existing in a realm above the changing world. The ultimate Ideas of the Good, the Beautiful and the True are what the philosopher directs himself to. He wishes to reach an area of thought and insight which transcends everyday thought and reality. But, as Nietzsche points out, these Ideas, as well as the means by which the philosopher attempts to gain insight into Reality and Truth have continually eluded the serious lover, the philosopher. He states that it is time to reformulate these ideals.

In *Thus Spoke Zarathustra*, Nietzsche describes three stages in understanding the nature of philosophical knowledge. Firstly, there is the stage of earnest searching for the truth. He calls this the stage of the camel, the beast of burden par excellence, who, significantly, lives in the desert. Secondly, there is the stage of the lion, the stage at which the philosopher focusses on the ideas of power and the will. Lastly, there is the stage at which one accepts the fact that the earnest searching for truth is an impossible ideal and one learns to live with this insight, joyful at the fact that one has reached this higher plane. Nietzsche calls this the stage of the child, the child who in its innocence approaches reality in a fresh way, allowing reality to show itself spontaneously. In its play, the child is not really concerned with whether the world it is creating is "real" or not: it is simply a reality in which the child lives at that moment. For Nietzsche, this notion of the playing child symbolises the activity of the philosopher.[9] In another description of these stages, Nietzsche uses the image of woman. The woman, in the final stage, is the image of truth, always veiling herself, always eluding the man chasing her, tempting him, withdrawing herself.[10]

These ideas are opposed to Plato's concept of truth. Nietzsche's view of truth can be seen as non-masculine or anti-masculine, a critique of Plato's identification of theoretical thought and the search for Ideas with a masculine order which excludes the feminine. Also opposed to Plato's philosophical insights is Nietzsche's view of truth as feminine as a positive appreciation of the earthly realm, of matters such as the love between man and woman, the family and reproduction. Nietzsche's ideas can be seen as positive for women because their nature and their approach to reality becomes the philosophical norm.[11]

On the other hand, allegorical figures of women are often deceptive, usually being less flattering than they appear to be at first sight. Nietzsche's idea of woman as truth or leading man to truth may seem attractive, but the reality is that the philosopher or the searcher for truth is male. He is the eager lover, he is ultimately the active subject. Nietzsche, as we saw, makes this clear in the passage from *Thus Spoke Zarathustra* on old and young women. In this passage, Nietzsche states that the highest ideal of a woman is to bear the Superman, the male who will be able to create new values for humankind. It is the Superman who has the subjectivity: the woman stands by, is image, means and object. The idea of subjectivity as masculine is also found in Nietzsche's use of a quotation from *Thus Spoke Zarathustra* in the *Genealogy of Morals*, a statement to the effect that Wisdom is a woman who only loves warriors.[12] Here too the male is the one fighting to find truth, the woman represents Wisdom and perhaps the elusiveness of the object of the warrior's search. The subjectivity of the feminine as a real-life woman is not referred to in this type of imagery.

The idea of woman as truth and as the beginning of a new feminine idea of truth is also perhaps not as new as Nietzsche claimed. As we have seen, Plato already identified women with sophistry and idle chatter. It seems that in a theory such as that of Nietzsche they are now allowed admission to the new male order of thought by being described in the old way. Some women simply want to be included in "serious thought", thus claiming for themselves both rationality and subjectivity. Others see Nietzsche as an ally, helping them to attack the objectifying and transcendent dimensions of male thought. But neither of these options are, when taken to their ultimate conclusion, very attractive. On the one hand, identification with the masculine means the absorption of the feminine within that order, without its own identity. On the other hand, conscious, subjective identification with the idea of the feminine as changing, perspectival, even sophistic may simply reinforce old prejudices and does not do justice to female thought. However one looks at these options, what is ultimately wrong with Nietzsche's imagery of the woman as truth is its absorption within exclusionary male subjectivity, seen as the only real activity. Women too are subjects involved with searching for truth, no matter how the truth and the road to finding truth is described.

6   Nietzsche and Feminism

Nietzsche, as may be concluded from his view of women as oriented towards love, men and the family, had a negative opinion of feminism. But, as is more often the case, his attitude seems ambiguous. During his professorship at the University of Basel, he did vote for the admission of female students to the university when presented with this issue in a committee he was on. This, however, could have been Nietzsche's irony and bitterness coming through because he did not think a great deal of his male colleagues. In fact, he had acrimonious debates with them and wrote a devastating critique of academia in *Thus Spoke Zarathustra*.[13] He may have thought that considering the lack of quality of males at the university it therefore did not mean a loss of prestige if it started admitting women. Yet this is pure speculation and there are other indications that Nietzsche in fact admired intellectual women, especially Lou Salomé, who so much desired a university education that she came all the way from Russia to Switzerland in order to find a university which would admit women.

Yet when it comes to the concrete issue of feminism, Nietzsche is very clear in his views. Moreover, his remarks concerning feminism are not made in passing, but reflect a number of central notions in his philosophy. One criticism of Nietzsche of feminism expresses a very central idea in his philosophy, that of the re-evaluation of all values. He states that feminists are devious women: they in fact attack other women by changing the values pertaining to women. Before feminism, women who were beautiful, attractive to men, loving, oriented to husband and family, stood in the highest regard with other women and with men. In feminism, Nietzsche argues, this situation is altered in the sense that a woman who was not successful at these things says that they are not important: the important things are matters such as getting a good education, fighting for social and political rights, being a free woman. The traditional woman with her traditional set of values is thus devalued by feminism with respect to both the male and the female traditional value systems. While previously women in traditional roles were the most successful and ranked highest in these systems, they are now looked down on by the new breed of feminists as catering to the male order and as not achieving enough within the new female one.

For Nietzsche, a fundamental critique of thought and society takes the form of re-evaluating values. This is the most effective instrument in dealing with people because it is the best instrument for gaining power over others.[14] Nietzsche says that the will to power is the most fundamental human impulse in our relationships with others and with reality. This means that feminism is simply, in its alteration of values, a will to power: a will to power not only over men but over "traditional" women as well.

Although for Nietzsche the idea of the will to power is pervasive and thus applicable to almost anything, his insight that feminism is a will to power is, I think, in some senses a very incisive and correct one. Feminism does seek to take some of the power away from the dominant male order which tends to impose its values on women, often to their detriment. What is interesting is that Nietzsche does not consider this point seriously, but rather emphasises the changes of values which occur among women themselves. This is of course a brilliant move, in the "divide and conquer" category. This attack on feminism is quite devastating in the sense that Nietzsche plays on the insecurity and guilt feelings of women. With this argument, he seeks to breed a feeling of doubt in feminists: perhaps they are not doing the right thing but are in fact attacking other women rather than fighting for the liberation of all women. In addition, the argument is effective in that it assumes without further ado that all feminists are unattractive and unsuccessful with men, playing out the old sexual theme and pumping female psychology in the manner already noted by Wollstonecraft half a century earlier. The assumption of the unattractiveness of feminists is smuggled in implicitly: it in fact reflects Nietzsche's values and the values of many men opposed to feminism and even of some women opposed to feminism. But a familiar pattern can be noted: the idea of "being attractive" is seen from out of a male perspective, without considering the subjectivity of the woman and her particular motivation for taking up a feminist position. For this reason, Nietzsche does not take feminism seriously as an intellectual, social or philosophical movement. In order to do that, he would have had to consider more specifically the views being discussed.

Another reason why Nietzsche did not take the feminist project seriously is because he saw the future salvation of the world in terms of a complete change of values from the Christian tradition towards a new, post-Christian order in which (superior) people would freely create their own values. The creation of a new society would, according to Nietzsche, be achieved when people have learned to express the positive nature of the will to power, the eternal return of the same, the love of life, and fate. The prophet Zarathustra's task was to announce the coming of the new values, the Superman was to bring them to life.[15] According to Nietzsche, only men have the power to create truly new values, only men have the moral and intellectual depth to have values at all. Nietzsche was aware of the fact that there were many social movements in his time: the demand for greater democracy and equal rights which had begun with the French Revolution, the worker's movements for better wages and working conditions. But all these were, in his view, banal in the sense that they tried to alter small parts of the social landscape but did not radically free society from its basic tendencies and values. He criticised movements for democracy and equal rights on the ground that they would bring about conformism: masses stamping their label of commonality on the rest of society. Such movements, Nietzsche feared, would create a society without art, without great intellectual pursuits, and without great achievements. Nietzsche calls for a return to the old aristocratic ideals in Europe. Nietzsche regards the aristocracy as the class which preserves culture, which rules in terms of its own good insights, which is truly "noble".[16]

Nietzsche's desire for a return to the old order, an order which he sees going back to the Greeks, goes against the social tendencies of his time.[17] Social movements such as feminism completely passed Nietzsche by. He was in fact fighting for an ideal of aristocracy which he saw as having been realised in its most noble form in ancient Greece, but which in fact had, literally and figuratively, been beheaded during the French Revolution and which would get its final, devastating blow in the years of war and revolution at the beginning of the 20th century.

7 Conclusions

There were a number of philosophers in the 19th century who saw the good sense of the women's movement. One could argue that this chapter has presented two bad examples of chauvenist philosophers. Perhaps more justice would have been done to the history of philosophy to have dealt with a "female-friendly" male 19th century philosopher. On the other hand, "female-friendly" philosophers may be less typical of 19th century philosophers than Schopenhauer and Nietzsche. One of the aims of this chapter is to show some of the reasons for the historical failure of 19th century philosophical literature to deal adequately with issues concerning women, issues such as those expressed by the women's liberation movement. While women were fighting for the right to an education, independence, the vote and equal rights, many 19th century philosophers were saying very different things about them. A number of the ideas discussed in this chapter are, I think, to most men as well as women, tedious in their banality and just plain embarassing. Written in an age which was still fairly naïve in terms of its awareness of psycho-sexual expression, they are expressions of basic urges by some men to see things in their own way. I think that the failure of 20th century male philosophers to deal adequately with women and women's issues is partly a result of 19th century failures in these matters, failures of, among others, Schopenhauer and Nietzsche.

But another factor in this failure is, I think, the social context in which 19th century philosophy began to develop, a development which continued in the 20th century. Philosophical discourse, including that on women, must be seen in light of the growth of universities and hence of academic philosophy in this period. Hegel, for example, the great professor at the University of Berlin, was given prestigious social status, a fact which Kierkegaard relates with distaste. Before this time, the majority of philosophers were people working on their own, not in academic settings. I think that this development had an impact on philosophical speaking about women. By making philosophy into work in a public, male sphere, with male status becoming an important factor, speaking about women was once more placed on the sidelines. Women were identified with the realm of the private, a realm to be left behind when working in the male-bonded sphere. If we add to this the 19th century failure to develop a coherent philosophical view on women, speaking about women came to be regarded as not proper, academic, or a particularly good idea. In a very important sense women came to be regarded as unimportant and non-existent.

It is, however, true that 19th century philosophers were not entirely swallowed up in the academic system. Schopenhauer and Nietzsche, the two philosophers discussed in this chapter, cannot of course be accused of being part of the male philosophical establishment. Schopenhauer failed to obtain a university position and Nietzsche gave up his relatively briefly held position at the University of Basel due to health reasons and difficulties with fellow academics. Precisely because of their feelings of exclusion, they did not have a high regard for academic philosophy and philosophers. Did their being excluded from a male-bonded system mean that they were more open to women and women's issues?[18] I think that in one respect this is the case. Nietzsche's view of woman as truth is a view of truth which indeed attempts to undermine systematic and dogmatic notions of truth. As I stated in my introduction to this book, Derrida was amazed that Martin Heidegger no longer deigned to mention Nietzsche's view of woman as truth, even though he analysed in painstaking detail all the other elements of Nietzsche's view of truth. This could well be a symptom of the difference in academic status and milieu of Heidegger and Nietzsche.

Nevertheless, it is then all the more discouraging that these two philosophers on the periphery of academia, for different reasons, saw no positive way to fight for a change in the image of women or for their liberation. Schopenhauer and Nietzsche were not in all respects the radical critics of 19th century society which they made themselves out to be. With regard to their views of women, they were in many ways typical of their time and in line with the tradition of philosophical thought. Their arguments are perhaps more strident than those of philosophers of the past, but the intellectual ingredients they use are as old as philosophy itself.

Unfortunately, these messages and lessons have failed to reach many male academics in the 20th century. Although written and unwritten academic codes of ethics forbid rabid attacks on certain people in society, including women, many philosophers today still think that it is possible to write a philosophical anthropology, a philosophy of politics or society, or an ethics, without the woman being present in any way. It can be argued, as such philosophers often do, that women are not a distinct social group or category and that therefore such a project is not necessary. A great deal of research has, however, shown that in many cases the word "person" as used by an author in fact means "male" and that women are in fact not being spoken about. In the next chapter, I will discuss one of the many contemporary female responses to the feeling of being excluded from philosophical discourse, as found in the work of L. Irigaray. Irigaray makes clear, in contrast to the "don't tell them what we think of them" patronising attitude of Nietzsche and the "they don't fit into male philosophical discourse" attitude of many philosophers today, that women have heard what men have said or not said about them, they have understood it, and want to put an end to it. Irigaray reflects the fact that women in the 20th century have for the first time had access to a university education and that they have become subjects of discourse and even silence themselves, not just objects. Hence the title of the next chapter: from différence to female speaking.

Notes

1   D. Spender, ed. *Feminist Theorists. Three Centuries of Key Women Thinkers.* New York/Toronto, Random House, 1983, includes essays on women activists of the 19th century and gives a good overview of this period.

2   A. Schopenhauer, *Essays and Aphorisms.* Selected and translated by R.J. Hollingdale. Harmondsworth, Middlesex, England, Penguin, 1970/1985, p. 80-88.

3   F. Nietzsche, *Zur Genealogie de Moral.* in: *Nietzsches Werke.* ed. by G. Stenzel. Salzburg, Bergland. Vol. 2, paragraph 7, p. 868-870. I will quote this passage here to illustrate how colourful the terms are in which Nietzsche expresses himself on this point: "Unterschätzen wir es namentlich nicht, dass Schopenhauer, der die Geschlecht-lichkeit in der Tat als persönlichen Feind behandelt hat (einbegriffen deren Werkzeug, das Weib, dieses "instrumentum diaboli"), Feinde nötig hatte, um guter Dinge zu bleiben; dass er die grimmigen, galligen, schwarzgrünen Worte liebte; dass er zürnte, um zu zürnen, aus Passion; dass er krank geworden wäre (-denn er war es nicht, so sehr er es auch wünschte) ohne seine Feinde, ohne Hegel, das Weib, die Sinnlichkeit und den ganzen Willen zum Dasein, Dableiben."

4   For discussions of Nietzsche's views on women, see: N. Malet, "L'homme et la femme dans la philosophie de Nietzsche". *Revue de Métaphysique et de Morale* 82 (1977, 1), p. 38-63; G. Ormiston, "Traces of Derrida: Nietzsche's Image of Woman". *Philosophy Today* (1984, Summer), p. 178-188; P. Patton, ed., *Nietzsche, Feminism and Political Theory.* London, Routledge, 1993.

5   F. Nietzsche, *Thus Spoke Zarathustra.* transl. by R.J. Hollingdale. London, Penguin, 1961/1969, p. 91-93.

6   F. Nietzsche, *Thus Spoke Zarathustra.* transl. by R.J. Hollingdale. London, Penguin, 1961/1969, p. 91 and 92-93.

7   H.F. Peters, *My Sister, My Spouse.* New York, Norton, 1962, describes the relationship between Nietzsche and Lou Salomé and has a reproduction of the photograph.

8   J. Derrida, Spurs/Éperons. *Nietzsche's Styles/Les Styles de Nietzsche.* Chicago/London, University of Chicago Press, 1978.

9   F. Nietzsche, *Thus Spoke Zarathustra.* transl. by R.J. Hollingdale. London, Penguin, 1961/1969, p. 54-56. (Of the Three Metamorphoses).

10 Another allegory of the feminine found in Nietzsche is his use of the symbol of Ariadne, the feminine figure who leads the male out of the labyrinth. See: Gilles Deleuze,

"Mystère d'Ariane" and Armand Quinot, "Ariane", in: *Bulletin de la Societé Française d'études Nietzschéennes* 2 (1963, mars), p. 12-15 and p. 16-18.

11 J. Derrida, *Spurs/Eperons. Nietzsche's Styles/Les Styles de Nietzsche.* (Chicago, Chicago University Press, 1978). See also: G. Ormiston, "Traces of Derrida: Nietzsche's Image of Woman", *Philosophy Today* (1984, Summer), p. 178-188.

12 F. Nietzsche, *Zur Genealogie der Moral*, in: F. Nietzsche, *Nietzsches Werke*. ed. by G. Stenzel. Salzburg, Bergland. Vol. II, p. 865. (motto of the Third Essay). Nietzsche writes: "Unbekümmert, spöttisch, gewalttätig – so will *uns* die Weisheit: sie ist ein Weib, sie liebt immer nur einen Kriegsmann"

13 F. Nietzsche, *Thus Spoke Zarathustra*. transl. by R.J. Hollingdale. London, Penguin, 1961/1969, p. 147. (Part II: Of Scholars)

14 F. Nietzsche, *Thus Spoke Zarathustra*. transl. by R.J. Hollingdale. London, Penguin, 1961/1969, p. 84-86. (Of the Thousand and One Goals). This theme is also central to F. Nietzsche, *Zur Genealogie der Moral*.

15 R.J. Hollingdale, "Introduction" to F. Nietzsche, *Thus Spoke Zarathustra*. transl. by R.J. Hollingdale. London, Penguin, 1961/1969, p. 11-35 gives a good background description of the nature and development of Nietzsche's concept of the Superman.

16 F. Nietzsche, *Zur Genealogie der Moral*, in: *Nietzsches Werke*. ed. by G. Stenzel. Salzburg, Bergland. Vol. 2, p. 832-835. (Part I, paragraph 10 and 11).

17 G.Lukács, *Die Zerstörung der Vernunft*. Berlin, Aufbau-Verlag, 1954. In this book, Lukács gives an extremely detailed analysis of the relationship between Nietzsche's philosophy and his reactionary views on social-political issues. For Lukács, the main purpose of such an analysis is to show Nietzsche's failure to deal with the problems of socialism (his book was written to support communist ideology). Although some of Lukács' views and criticisms of Nietzsche may be called excessive, other points he makes are on the mark and also applicable to Nietzsche's views on feminism.

18 Annelies van Heijst, *Verlangen naar de val*, Kampen, Kok, 1992, p. 64-67. Van Heijst argues that "*randmannen*", which can roughly be translated as "men on the periphery", can be valuable allies for the development of feminist theory.

9 L. Irigaray. From Différence to Female Speaking.

1 Introduction

In this chapter, I would like to look at one of the most creative and interesting of contemporary philosophers who discuss questions surrounding the masculine and feminine, Luce Irigaray (1930).[1] The main theme of this chapter will be the search by women for their own voice, their own subjectivity, in the communicaton community which is our culture. Irigaray demonstrates that women have always been excluded from the process of speaking by the dominance of male perspectives and the male perception that a woman is not really present. She attempts to present a positive alternative to this state of affairs in which the female is actuality, presence, reality, and speech in her own right.

Irigaray studied linguistics and philosophy at the University of Louvain in Belgium, writing a Ph.D. thesis on Paul Valéry. She taught for a while and then moved to Paris to study psychopathology at the University of Paris. Her second Ph.D. thesis, *Le langage des déments*, on the use of language by the mentally disturbed, was published in 1973. She then worked on her *doctorat d'état*, the state doctorate which would give her access to a permanent teaching position, by writing her first full-fledged feminist psychology/philosophy book, *Speculum, de l'autre femme* (*Speculum. Of the Other woman*), published in 1974. This book created a furor in the examining committee, but was eventually accepted. Three weeks later, however, she was fired from the University of Vincennes. She had alienated people from the school of Jacques Lacan.[2] She could, however, keep her job at the Centre National de la Recherche Scientifique (National Center for Scientific Research), allowing her to continue her academic work. She set up a psychoanalytical practice in her home in Paris, where she still lives. She has her own students and followers, and has written a considerable number of books and given lectures at many universities. Among the books she has published are readings of Nietzsche, Heidegger, works dealing with ethics, female forms of expression, critiques of sexism in philosophy and the sciences. She has received invitations from universities around the world to give guest lectures and seminars.[3]

In this chapter, I will concentrate mainly on the most surprising of Irigaray's works in terms of its originality, *Speculum*. In her later work, Irigaray follows up on the themes and methodology begun in *Speculum*, developing new ideas and perspectives from out of this first book. The book begins with a critique of Freud's view of women, proceeds to a critique of sexism in the history of philosophy, dealing with Plato, Aristotle, the medieval mystical tradition, Descartes, Kant and Hegel. She ends the book with a detailed discussion of Plato, concentrating on his allegory of the cave. I will first give some examples of Irigaray's philosophical approach in *Speculum* and in the final part of the chapter, I will look at some theoretical issues raised by Irigaray's philosophy, concentrating on the equality-difference debate, the most pressing debate on the role and status of women in society today.

2   Irigaray's Reading of Freud

Irigaray, in speaking of *Speculum*, states that there is no beginning or end to the book.[4] She begins with a detailed discussion of Freud but the fact she begins *Speculum* in this way is not arbitrary. As a psychologist and philosopher, Irigaray wants to investigate the masculine biases in Freud's theories in order to lay the groundwork for a much broader philosophical-historical look at the preconceptions and prejudices which men have about women. In her view, Freud's theories on women are not so much a diagnosis of the nature of women as they are themselves symptoms of what is wrong with the way men think about women. In order to demonstrate this, Irigaray "reads" texts by Freud on women.[5] By saying that she reads the texts, I mean that she follows the words and images in the text to find what dynamics lie behind their use, what presuppositions colour the order of Freud's discourse. In this way, Irigaray does not present a distanced, analytical or clinical approach but she simply allows the sexist implications of images and theories to emerge.

For Irigaray, Freud's theory of female sexuality and sexual development is symptomatic of male speech concerning women for a number of reasons. Firstly, she cites the pattern we have also seen repeated in almost all the texts discussed in this book of taking up an explicitly male perspective, of "we" versus "them". For example, Freud asks his readers and listeners to examine the mystery of women, assuming that his audience is male. Freud uses the "conspiratorial" tactic which Plato and Nietzsche also use. For example, he states a number of so-called characteristics of women and he notes that if a woman hears of this and objects, one is to respond with the reassurance, "But, my dear, *you* are an exception and not like that".[6]

Secondly, there is the pattern of seeing women as a vaguer, lesser "mirror" of the ideal characteristics of men. Freud expresses ideas similar to Aristotle's view of the female as a defective male, as "lack" and passivity. Freud, to his credit, states that looking at the female in terms of these categories will not really advance the science of understanding women. But, as Irigaray points out, his entire theory of female sexuality supports the idea of the female as defect, lack, and passivity. This lack is expressed specifically in the female lack of the male sexual organ. To understand how Freud comes to the conclusion that the female is lack, it is necessary to look at his view of male and female sexual development.

According to Freud, children up to the age of three develop their sexual orientation through their association with the male and the female, usually portrayed by their parents. In the case of the female child, Freud states that in the first period of her development, the girl feels she resembles her mother. She soon recognises, however, the disadvantages of such an identification. The mother is not only a rival to the daughter for the love of the father, but, even worse, the daughter gradually realises that the mother does not have a penis, the organ denoting the power and superiority of the male. According to Freud, a young girl becomes aware of the penis by seeing it on a brother or other young boys. The realisation that she and her mother lack this means the young girl turns away in disappointment from the penisless mother and strives for the love of the father. The father will, normally, reject the girl so that she starts to desire a male of her own. After that, she will desire a male child, a bearer of the penis she misses. This rather incredible story centred on the male organ serves the purpose on a more banal level of defining the female purpose in life as oriented to and appropriating the male.

According to Freud, female sexual development is much more complex than male sexual development for two reasons. These two reasons are also, according to Freud, explanations for why females suffer from "hysterical" symptoms. Firstly, the female cannot express her natural aggression in the same way that a male can. Freud states that young boys and girls have an equal amount of aggression but that the boy can live out that aggression, while in the case of the girl, oriented as she is to obtaining the love of the father and other men in her life, it is necessary to suppress this aggression. The girl must not only come to accept the fact that she has no penis and must create her own identity through another, but in order to become a woman she must develop passivity. On the sexual level, this passivity means that becoming a woman implies transferring the pleasure given by the clitoris, the shrunken male organ of the female, into true feminine, vaginal pleasure. Such a process involves accepting sexual passivity as well as social passivity: she comes to realise that she can only obtain a man through passive behaviour.

The second respect in which the male and female differ is that while the male may retain his bonding with his mother in his adult life, combining it with his love for a wife, the woman must, in order to orient herself to the male, completely cut off her relationship with the mother. As Irigaray notes, this is a curious theory because it breaks with the symmetry of Freud's analyses of the development of the two genders. Why does Freud suddenly analyse the male's relationship to the mother differently from the female's? Irigaray argues that this is an attempt by Freud to take away the "origin" and "history" from the female since the male retains his origin, the female not. She argues the male always wants to appropriate to himself the cluster discourse-economy-desire.

Taking away the history of the woman takes away the roots of her identity and also, according to Irigaray, her roots in discourse. Irigaray argues that female hysteria, one of the major areas of Freud's research, is not diagnosed properly by him precisely because it is caused by the male order itself, of which Freud's own views are an example. Female hysteria originates in the woman's exclusion from the realm of discourse. A woman's only recourse becomes non-verbal protest. Irigaray links the terms hysteria/mystery because "mystery" is another basic term which Freud uses to describe the feminine. The mystery of women lies in the fact that men do not understand them. This is, according to Irigaray, a point of view which is itself the result of the woman being excluded from her origins and language.

Freud himself realised that his understanding of female sexuality was not a complete or clear one, calling women a mystery, a riddle.[7] Irigaray concludes that this is not a positive point of departure for Freud's

attempt to understand women. She argues that the main barrier to
Freud's understanding of women is his male perspective which does not
allow him to think of female sexuality in terms of being its own type of
sexuality. In Freud's view, female sexuality is a lack. The woman has
"no" organs of her own, apart from the shrivelled male organ. Female
sexual organs are for the rest "nothing". Her origin and purpose in life,
defined in terms of male structures and desires, is also "nothing" of its
own.

In her critique of Freud, Irigaray notes that any disappointment the
girl may feel with the mother may say more about how males view
females, about the sexual power relationship between them, and about
social norms rather than about presumed defects in female sexuality.[8]
Manhood involves not just a certain type of sexual apparatus but
designates male superiority, freedom, opportunity and domination. The
idea that penis envy occurs in women is not an empirically verified fact
and most likely untrue.[9] Instead, this idea is most likely a symbolical
expression of the realities of powerlessness and repression of women in
Freud's Vienna and many other places in 19th century Europe.

3   Subjectivity Appropriated to the Masculine

In Part II of *Speculum,* Irigaray examines sexism in the history of
philosophy and psychoanalyses structures of philosophical thought. She
demonstrates that sexism is in fact rampant in the history of philosophy.
In arguing this, she comes up with a plethora of ideas, images, and values
linked by philosophers to male and female.

Irigaray opens Part II with a chapter in which she argues that in
philosophical thought subjectivity has always been appropriated to the
masculine. She illustrates this theme by using the image of the Ptolemaic
system being replaced by the Copernican. The image of the Copernican
revolution is an image already used in the 18th century by Kant and
applied by other philosophers such as Ernst Cassirer to describe the
move to modernity in philosophical thought and philosophical anthropology. Irigaray applies this image to a re-evaluaton or transformation
of the traditional male-female distinction as made in philosophy. Philosophical thought has always and is still revolving around one pole, the
male who originates it and about whom it speaks. The earth, the

feminine, should not be seen as revolving as a lesser entity around the sun (Apollo, reason), but in fact, according to Irigaray, it turns on itself.[10] In other words, female reality does not revolve around the male nor can it be described as a weak reflection of the male. This is the revolutionary idea which, according to Irigaray, must be introduced into contemporary philosophy, one that has not yet occurred in the progression of the "male imaginary" towards modernity.

Traditionally in philosophical thought, the male sees himself as symbolising reason and transcendence, while he sees the female as symbolising immanence, nature and matter. The male does not realise that he cannot, in this way, define and capture the feminine. As the male seeks for truth and reality higher above the earth, he is unable to come to terms with the earth. If he persists in shutting himself off from the feminine, he loses his own link to the earth, his own roots and identity. The male seeks to see everything in terms of the economy of the same, to reduce his understanding of something which is essentially "other" to a pale mirroring of himself. This, however, is not possible. The feminine, especially to a masculine which has distanced itself from it, is truly other, has become ungraspable. Reason, "objectivity", will not give the desired result: the male must reopen his mind to the realms of thought which have been repressed by rationality, those of dreams and the unconscious. The feminine exists in a world of a different syntax, another type of meaning. As opposed to the cool rationality of thought, it is concrete and burns up male rationality.

After this introductory statement describing the philosophical context in which she will develop her philosophical views, Irigaray discusses a number of texts from the history of philosophy. I will discuss as an example of her approach her reading of Plato's allegory of the cave.

4   Plato's Allegory of the Cave

The final part of *Speculum* deals with Plato's allegory of the cave. The allegory, denoting the road one must take from ignorance to knowledge, is, according to Irigaray, full of imagery Freud would recognise. The story, briefly, is as follows. There are a number of men tied up in a cave. They have their backs to the opening of the cave and are facing a wall with a fire in front of it. On the wall, shadows of things are being

projected. One of the prisoners manages to free himself and to walk out
of the cave into the sun. At first he is blinded by seeing things in the
sun but he becomes used to it. He then goes back into the cave and tells
the others about the things he has seen but he is rejected by them. For
Plato, the allegory of the cave symbolises the struggle to attain true
knowledge through philosophical thought rather than remaining in the
sphere of mere opinion. Following the story of the cave, Plato writes on
the importance of education.[11]

Applying a Freud-used-against-himself analysis, Irigaray interprets
the cave as the womb in which men feel imprisoned, the opening of the
cave as the birth canal. She argues that men (as Freud also thought) have
the basic need to break off their early identification with their mother.
This early bond is a biological bond: men are born of women and first
identify with the mother because she cares for them. But in order to
become a man, the young boy must identify himself with the father
through the Oedipus complex. Irigaray concludes that men have a fear
of being shut in, imprisoned by the womb (or later, by the vagina).

The process of breaking off the identification with the female and
entering into the male world is symbolised by Plato by the process of
attaining knowledge and doing philosophy. Plato uses male images for
knowledge: it is symbolised by the appearance of things in the sun.[12]
Linked to these images is a value system of the higher and the lower,
the superior and the inferior, inner and outer, darkness and light,
ignorance and knowledge, categories by which men give more status to
their side than to that of the female.

The conclusion of this psychoanalysis of Plato's allegory of the cave
is that the attainment of knowledge and the doing of philosophy is a
process of male bonding in which males create their own symbolical
order to the exclusion of the feminine. Knowledge is not something
which is obtained "for itself" but is an instrument in the process of
coming to gender self-identification.

Throughout *Speculum*, Irigaray gives many examples of male
thought and imagery in philosophy by describing how male philosophers think: the doing of metaphysics to reach a higher, nobler male
realm above that of female everyday life; the striving of males to identify
with a self-projected male order of the divine; the search by males for
clear and distinct knowledge, presumably opposed to female irrationality and unclarity; the priority of male desires for form, reason, action

and control above female matter, emotion and passivity; and the urge to order and control reality and the feminine by "placing" the feminine in certain categories, by "setting" certain goals, ideals and ends for the feminine. As to female imagery in philosophy, the feminine is associated with the natural, the cyclical, the realms of the earth, the family and reproduction.

For Irigaray, the most fundamental "given" at the basis of these types of images is the sexual, in the sense of physical-sexual reality. For example, Irigaray sees a link between the male sexual organ and the sex act and notions of teleology and control, between female physiology and sexual reaction and notions of the diffuse and holistic. Sexuality is based on physiological reactions which, in her view, can be associated with characteristics of male and female thought.

5   Deconstruction and Mimesis

Although we have seen that Irigaray comes to very forceful results in her reading of Freud and the history of philosophy, it is not the case that Irigaray uses a methodology in the traditional sense or that she describes systematically or abstractly what she is doing and what the results are. Such an approach would, in her own eyes, mean that she is using the methodology of male thought, while her intention is to present an alternative to such thought. I have already indicated that Irigaray uses a "reading" approach, which can be linked to the psychoanalytic approach of letting the patient go through a process of free association in order to reveal the nature of the neurosis. In this sense, even though she criticises Freud, Irigaray makes use of some of his techniques. Besides a psychoanalytic approach in her work, there is also a philosophical one. Two aspects of this philosophical approach are deconstruction and mimesis.

Irigaray calls her philosophy deconstructive in the sense that she, like Heidegger (whose term this is) wishes to present a critique of the western philosophical tradition but realises that she herself is working within the conceptual framework of that tradition. No thinker, both Irigaray and Heidegger realise, can start entirely anew from a point outside the tradition itself. This ambiguous aspect of borrowing from tradition and presenting a critique of it is expressed by the term deconstruction. A number of images have been used to explain this term. One can think of the Baron Munkhausen image of rebuilding a boat board by board while it is floating on the water. Another image used is that of breaking down a house from within, destroying the foundations without the walls falling down on one. In essence, both images express the idea of using philosophical material against itself or of placing oneself within that to which one is opposed.[13]

The philosophical image of deconstruction goes remarkably well with the psychoanalytic approach. In therapy, the analyst just lets the patient talk, not by asking questions from out of some different, theoretical context, but from out of the terminology, ideas and images used by the patient. Understanding comes to the patient by realising what he or she is expressing.

Although Heidegger and Irigaray have differing styles, both see the issue as one of asking what philosophers (or, if you will, western thought) are really *saying*. Heidegger does this through depth analyses and etymologies of the terms philosophers use, Irigaray through a process of the association of ideas. Irigaray, like Heidegger, is not overly concerned with more academic types of interpretation. In Irigaray's texts it is sometimes difficult to distinguish who is speaking, the philosopher in question or Irigaray the deconstructivist and psychoanalyst. Irigaray refuses to use footnotes or bibliographies: the process of thinking and writing is not one of distanced analysis but of intense conversation. Although she develops a different kind of "philosophy of difference" than Jacques Derrida, she is, like him, concerned with the way in which language expresses meaning and thought. Derrida expands Heidegger's deconstructive approach to language by asking what language implicitly and explicitly expresses by means of a social-psychological reading of texts.[14] Irigaray uses the same kind of technique as Derrida of looking at the contexts and connotations of the use of terms and images as well as reading between the lines, asking questions as to the points jumped over by the author in the text, the seemingly illogical moves which the philosopher makes to hide or express ideas.

Another term which Irigaray uses to describe her approach is taken from Aristotle: mimesis. Mimesis has a number of meanings but can be loosely translated as mimicry. For Aristotle, mimesis is at the heart of art and literature because they mimic reality. For Irigaray, mimesis means mimicing sexism in philosophical texts. Again, mimicry is not critique from outside, but from inside a view or a theory. But the repetition is not pure reproduction. The repetition is just "off", just "different enough" to show where the gaps are, where the sexism lies. For Irigaray, women mimicing male chauvinism is effective in the sense that it gives them the opportunity to demonstrate their irony and to allow room for laughter, that is, to show (one can think here of the Wittgensteinian notion of "showing" as opposed to "saying") how wrong and ridiculous sexism is. The more women repeat the prejudices, the less men will take the ideas they previously held seriously.

6   Positive Philosophy

Besides presenting a critique of male thought, Irigaray's aim is to re-think and re-express female sexuality and reality. Irigaray argues against Freud that it is necessary to express female sexuality in its own terms. The female of course has her own sexual organs and sexual experiences which males may find puzzling over against a male sexuality which is more directed to its object. She speaks of a holistic, diffuse female sexuality. Women have most likely always been aware of the fact that they are not "nothing" or "lack" in the Aristotelian and Freudian sense. The time has come, in an age in which women have been able to enter into traditionally exclusive male realms of arts, sciences and academia, to express the positive ways in which they differ from the masculine. On all levels, women should express the "difference" between male and female as a truly fundamental difference. This time, the difference will not be the difference spoken of by male thinkers where difference implies inferiority, but a difference between two distinct genders, each having their own value. Applying this notion of difference to a cultural and artistic level, Irigaray urges women to express themselves in areas such as philosophy, science, art, and literature. In philosophy there is a great need for women to begin to write and express their own perspective. Irigaray feels that she herself has started on this road, calling her own philosophical writing *écriture féminin*, female writing. Female expression will be flowing, diffuse, earthy and earthly, and, to men, confusing and perhaps nonsensical because men will, as in the case of Freud, be unable to grasp the feminine content. If, Irigaray says, female thought and writing leads to male confusion, it means that it has successfully broken with male thought and writing, which is a writing which only accepts an "economy of the self-same".[15]

7   Equality and Difference

The ideas of Irigaray have had a great impact on women's studies in philosophy, providing it with a very interesting and pronounced approach. A number of discussions have arisen about her views, but it seems to me that the most important one concerns her idea of difference. The idea that there is a very fundamental difference between male and female, masculinity and femininity lies at the basis of her philosophy in both its criticism of male thought and in its attempt to create a positive new notion of the feminine. But "is" there a fundamental and to a large extent "natural" difference between men and women? Are these differences so fundamental that one can speak of male and female thought? What difference *would* it have made if women had always been included in the intellectual development of western society? Is gender and sexuality so fundamental that they give men and women different natures? Can one extrapolate from the sexual and from sexual characteristics to intellectual and cultural areas?

There are two ways of approaching these questions: firstly, in terms of the philosophical status of the idea of difference and secondly, in terms of the social-political implications of difference thinking.

On the philosophical level, the accusation can been levelled at Irigaray of introducing a form of biologism. Biology seems to play a large role in the formation of the intellectual concepts of which she speaks and biologism is notoriously difficult to prove. Irigaray is herself aware of such criticism, stating that she never intended to produce a biological theory.[16] Indeed, biologism is not a very appropriate basis for her philosophy since it carries with it connotations of determinism. If men had been determined by their sexuality to produce the type of thought which they have, then any criticism of that or the call for a new male mentality would be quite pointless. But by noting the parallels between the biological differences between male and female and the patterns in which sexism is expressed in philosophy, she does not want to reduce matters to a physicalist notion of human nature or determinism through nature. Still, however one describes her approach, this remains a difficulty in her philosophy.

A second philosophical point which has been made concerning Irigaray's idea of difference is that almost without exception the male chauvenist philosophers whom she discusses and criticises have worked with a notion of difference, one often based on a presupposition that there are naturally given human characteristics. Irigaray, however, claims that her notion of difference is not the same as those used in the philosophical tradition. For her, difference is a positive notion, not one of "superiority-inferiority" or "complementarity" (the two patterns most often found in the philosophical literature). In addition, and I think this is for Irigaray the most important point, it is now women themselves who are saying how they differ: women have become "subjects" of philosophical discourse instead of "objects" being de-scribed by men. Still, apart from the reasonableness of Irigaray's alter-native notion of difference, feminists have stated that maintaining a notion of difference still carries with it the problem of what I would like to call the "feminine ghetto", that is, that a strong notion of difference leads to an expression of "otherness" which begins to live a relatively isolated life, isolated from "masculine thought" and women who are still willing to participate in that. The "ghetto" idea expresses the fact that, despite all the efforts by feminists they are, always and ever again, considered to be "different" and even "inferior", on the "fringe" of the dominant order. The notion of positive difference together with inte-gration is a very high ideal. The question is which strategy women should use to deal with the dominant order: difference and equality or sameness and equality?

This leads to the second set of objections which have been made to Irigaray's notion of difference, what I would like to call the "liberal" objection. Going back to Mary Wollstonecraft and much of the feminist tradition of the 19th century up to the birth of the "second wave" of feminism dating from the 1960's, many women have said that the main goal is to achieve equality with men. On this view, men and women are not fundamentally different, but if there are any differences, this fact must be considered to be secondary to the fact that they are in the first place human beings. It can be argued that gender differences are about as relevant in dealing with the notion of human nature as skin colour is. The fundamental sameness is so overriding that it would be improper to speak of difference in any fundamental sense.

Some of the philosophers discussed in this book have discussed the issue of the fundamental sameness of people and the secondary nature of gender differences. Rousseau and Kant, for example, explicitly deal with this question, as do Aquinas and the Christian tradition. Are we not, male and female, all human beings? The problem with the views of these philosophers, as we have seen, is, however, that they claim that there are really quite relevant differences between men and women, differences which mean that they should be treated or educated in different ways. In this sense, as we have seen, the notion of sameness of male and female and a communal basis in human nature is often ambiguous in the western philosophical tradition.

In the feminist "liberal" tradition, the idea of the sameness of human nature is associated with complete equality. Wollstonecraft, as we saw, came to this conclusion in a very pronounced way in her critique of Rousseau. The feminist view of sameness as fundamental leads to a new view of the feminine, of philosophical thought, and of equal rights. Women see this concept as the basis for overcoming exclusion in all areas of life and thought. Irigaray explicitly rejects this option, saying that women will again be selling themselves out and sacrificing their identities to "masculine thought" with which, she argues, all women in academic spheres have been or can be infected.

Another aspect of the difference-sameness debate is on the social-political level. Do both genders have the same social rights and privileges and should both conform to the same standards in society? The debate concerning sameness and difference has coloured much of feminist discussion in the political arena. The "liberal" thinkers have argued that they have a consistent and strong position: equal natures means equal rights. The difference thinkers say that equality thinkers have an image of people as androgynous creatures, denying the reality and needs of male and female identities and the positive contributions both can make from out of their difference. But this position makes the thinkers of "difference", such as Irigaray, vulnerable to the accusation that they lack commitment to fundamental equality. The difference side responds to this by saying that in the equality position women will loose their own identity[17]. Perhaps a very simple example of this debate on the social-political level concerns the workplace. Should men and women be held

to the same standards, have the same rights, and earn the same salaries
for the same work? Or should women be given additional rights, for
example, pregancy leave and time for raising children and caring for a
young family? Such a difficult issue as this shows how complicated it is
to make decisions about sameness and difference between men and
women: human rights should also be based on needs. A very important
point to note, however, is that difference thinkers do not have as solid
a basis in an idea of shared human nature which liberals have; it is a
"postmodern", more fragile and fragmentary view than the Enlightenment position.[18] The balance of power between equality thinkers and
difference thinkers will, I think, keep swinging from one side to the
other. This is because they are not merely expressing intellectual fashions, but they are responding to changing social and economic situations
and demands. After all, the concern behind this debate is how women
function in the family and the workplace, situations which are influenced by social and economic factors and which are of vital concern
both to individuals and to society. Women and society tend to shift
focus on equality or difference, as was the case for example in the 1940's
("equality" for the war effort) and the 1950's ("difference" for putting
women back in the home). Perhaps now, in the 1990's, as a response to
the equality thinking of the 1960's to 1980's, there is once more a
movement towards difference thinking such as expressed by Irigaray.
This contemporary form of difference thinking is, however, often
thought to be based on equality as guaranteed by society. In the final
chapter of this book, besides drawing conclusions from the discussions
held of the philosophers discussed in this book, I will also attempt to
analyse the very complicated social phenomenon of feminism in the
1990's.

Notes

1 L.D. Derksen, "Luce Irigaray. Het denken van differentie", H.E.S. Woldring, ed.,
   Moderne franse filosofen. Kampen, Kok, 1993, p. 46-63, is an earlier version of this
   chapter.

2 K. Amsberg and A. Steenhuis, Interview with L. Irigaray, "Al eeuwen lang leven wij
   in de verhouding moeder-zoon", in: *Denken over liefde en macht*. Amsterdam, van

Gennep, 1982, p. 113-127. The interviewers added a brief curriculum vitae of Luce Irigaray, p. 114-116.

3 For a list of Irigaray's works, see the bibliography at the end of this book.

4 L. Irigaray, *This Sex Which Is Not One*. transl. by C. Porter with C. Burke. Ithaca, Cornell University Press, 1985, p. 68.

5 L. Irigaray, *Speculum. Of the Other Woman*. transl. by Gillian C. Gill. Ithaca, New York, Cornell University Press, 1985, p. 13-129. For the texts Irigary reads, see: S. Freud, *The Standard Edition of the Complete Psychological Works of Sigmund Freud*. ed. by J. Strachey. London, Hogarth Press, 1953-1974, 24 vols. The specific sources are cited in footnotes in the English edition only.

6 S. Freud, *The Standard Edition of the Complete Psychological Works of Sigmund Freud*. ed. by J. Strachey. London, Hogarth Press, 1953-1974. "Femininity", in Volume 22, p. 116-117. L. Irigaray, *Speculum. Of the Other Woman*. transl. by Gillian C. Gill. Ithaca, Cornell University Press, 1985, p. 23.

7 S. Freud, *The Standard Edition of the Complete Psychological Works of Sigmund Freud*. ed. by J. Strachey. London, Hogarth Press, 1953-1974. "Femininity", in Volume 22, p. 113. L. Irigaray, *Speculum. Of the Other Woman*. transl. by Gillian C. Gill. Ithaca, Cornell University Press, 1985, p. 13.

8 L. Irigaray, *Speculum. Of the Other Woman*. transl. by Gillian C. Gill. Ithaca, New York, Cornell University Press, 1985, p. 50-53, and L. Irigaray, *This Sex Which Is Not One*. transl. by C. Porter with C. Burke. Ithaca, New York, Cornell University Press, 1985, p. 23-33, 34-67.

9 L. Irigaray, *Speculum. Of the Other Woman*. transl. by Gillian C. Gill. Ithaca, Cornell University Press, 1985, p. 50-53. See also: William P. Alston, "Psychoanalytic Theories, Logical Status of", in: *The Encyclopedia of Philosophy*. ed. by P. Edwards. New York/London, MacMillan and the Free Press/Collier MacMillan, 1967. Vol. 6, p.512-516.

10 In fact, this image is fairly complicated. In the Ptolemaic system, the earth (in Irigaray's terms, the feminine) is considered to be the center of the universe and the sun (the masculine for Irigaray) revolves around it. Irigaray would not want to say that this image reflects the views on men and women in the history of philosophy. In the Copernican system, the earth revolves around the sun. This is a clearer image of the sexism which Irigaray wishes to reveal. For Kant and Cassirer, the Copernican image demonstrates the decentralisation of man: man no longer stands at the center of the universe. For Irigaray, it is time to say in a different way that males no longer stand in the center of reality; the female no longer revolves around the male. It is in this sense that I interpret Irigaray's statement that the full implications of a modern view of man and woman still needs to be implemented.

11 Plato, *Collected Dialogues*. transl. by Hamilton and Cairns. Princeton, Princeton University Press, 1961, p. 749-753. *Republic* VII, 517a-521a.

12 In Greek thought, the sun is a male image, associated with reason, Apollo is the god of the sun and reason. The moon and earth (in Plato's case a dark cave) are associated with the female, Demeter is the goddess of the earth. Both these gods can both be linked to the birth place of western philosophy, Delphi, where Socrates, so the story goes, received his philosophical mission. In the course of time, Demeter was replaced as goddess of Delphi by Apollo.

13 L. Irigaray. *This Sex Which Is Not One*. transl. by C. Porter with C. Burke. Ithaca, New York, Cornell University Press, 1985, p. 144-148, 150-152. See also: E. Echeverria, *Criticism and Commitment. Major Themes in Contemporary 'Post-Critical' Philosophy.* Amsterdam, Rodopi, 1981.

14 For a very clear analysis of the influence of Heidegger on Derrrida and on Derrida's innovations on Heidegger's notion of deconstruction, see: G.C. Spivak, "Translator's Preface" to J. Derrida, *On Grammatology*. Baltimore/London, Johns Hopkins University Press, 1974, 1976. p. ix-xc.

15 L. Irigaray, *Speculum. Of the Other Woman*. transl. by Gillian C. Gill. Ithaca, New York, Cornell University Press, 1985, p.26-27, 32-34, 42-44. and L. Irigaray, *This Sex Which Is Not One*. transl. by C. Porter with C. Burke. Ithaca, New York, Cornell University Press, 1985, p. 23-33.

16 L. Irigaray, *This Sex Which Is Not One*. transl. by C. Porter with C. Burke. Ithaca, Cornell University Press, 1985. This book contains a number of interviews with Irigaray in which she speaks of her theoretical approach.

17 L. Irigaray, *Je, tu, nous: pour une culture de la différence*. Paris, Editions Grasset et Fasquelle, 1990. English translation: *Je, tu, nous: Towards a Culture of Difference*. New York, Routledge, 1993. In this book, Irigaray warns repeatedly against the threat of the loss of feminine identity in a society focussed on undifferentiated equality. She states that she is even willing to sacrifice gains made in social equality (in the job market, e.g.) in order to allow women to have space to be themselves. She also gives explicit instructions as to how to strengthen the female sense of identity, especially in the relationships between female friends and between mother and daughter.

18 For more detailed discussions concerning the modernism-postmodernism debate in feminism see: L. Nicholson, ed. *Feminism/Postmodernism*. New York/London, Routledge, 1990, and M. Pellikaan-Engel, ed., *Against Patriarchal Thinking*. Amsterdam, VU University Press, 1992, p. 131-209.

10 Conclusions. Women, Nature and Culture

1 Introduction

In this book, I have described various images of women and ideas concerning roles for women as they are presented by some of the main thinkers in the history of philosophy. For me, the most surprising result of this research is the fact that so much of what has been said about women in the philosophical tradition is "the same". By "the same" I mean that philosophers, when speaking about women, leave no cliché unturned. Women are seen as less rational than men, belong in the home, and are to be excluded from the public and intellectual life of society. The female is seen as functioning within and symbolically representing the cyclical, natural order, the male as standing for and achieving things in the historical, cultural order. With respect to the male order, that of the female is inferior. The Pythagorean women, Plato, Aristotle, Aquinas, Bacon, Rousseau, Kant, Schopenhauer and Nietzsche are all to some extent of this opinion. Plato is the only philosopher on this list who wanted to break out of this pattern, but as we saw, his efforts are at best ambiguous.

Some of the other philosophers discussed, Christine de Pizan, Descartes, and Mary Wollstonecraft, have in common a desire to increase the scope of the concept of human nature and to see women as equal to men and as being capable of achievements in the realms traditionally called male. Irigaray is perhaps in her own category, in that she wishes to reformulate the question of the relationship between a general concept of human nature and the valuation of the masculine and feminine by combining the notions of difference and equality.

As Plato and Aristotle already indicated, the main point around which the gender discussion revolves concerns the view of the nature of women and their role in society. Are men and women "naturally" "the same" or are they "different"? If men and women can be seen as having their own "natural" characteristics, what does that say about their roles in society? Should men and women have different/unequal or the same/equal social status and roles? Should we follow Irigaray's sugges-tion that there be a positive appreciation in society of femininity as "different"? Or should we see male and female as different from each other but at the same time as having "equal" human and social rights in a political and legal sense? Or should we make use of other theoretical models to express the relationship between the two genders? For example, a promising area might be that of the study of the social and political aspects of modern pluralism in philosophy and anthropology. Could we describe male and female as different "cultures" which should be treated in light of an ethics of pluralism?

Underlying these questions is another question. How can we separate our views of male and female nature from the socialisation processes in which such views take shape? And perhaps the deepest question is: why do humans make so many distinctions and judgments concerning the ideology of gender in the first place?

In this concluding chapter, I would like to discuss the nature-culture distinction as it applies to the creation of male-female images and give the beginning of an answer to the question of why humans make ideological distinctions between males and females.

2   Nature, Culture and Society

Traditionally, there are two possible approaches to answering questions about how human beings come to be the way they are. One can take a historical-cultural point of view, seeing human beings as formed by socialisation processes and analysing the valuation and exclusion of individuals in cultural contexts. One can also take nature as the point of departure, searching for the reasons for the way we are in human nature, biology and instincts. In this book, dealing as it does with the history of ideas, cultural aspects of the valuation of the male and female have been discussed. Yet, as we also saw in this book, the concept of human nature, male and female nature, is very important to philosophers because "nature" can function as a foundation and therefore as a justification for certain "cultural" views. To some extent, all the philosophers we have discussed revert to a notion of human nature as underlying speaking about male and female on a cultural level. The appeal to a foundation in nature for cultural conclusions is expressed most clearly by Aristotle. For him, a social order is a "correct" order when it reflects the natural characteristics of those participating in it. For Plato, there is a link between natural characteristics and social roles, but in a weaker sense than for Aristotle. As Plato states in the *Republic*, it is at least theoretically possible to reconsider ideas concerning the nature of people, a process which implies the possibility of a reconsideration of the existing social order. Conservative thinkers such as Aristotle tend to put more emphasis on human nature and natural characteristics in order to strengthen their presuppositions about male and female. Thinkers such as Plato who are open to alternative ideas and the possibility of change in the way society operates will argue that "natural" characteristics may be socially coloured and hence subject to reinterpretation in different social contexts.

I think that we can draw two conclusions from the nature-culture discussions we have encountered in this book. Firstly, nature and culture are both important factors in forming people. Through socialisation, we become human, that is, we develop the capacity to experience human feelings, to respond to people and situations in typically human ways, to reason and use language to express ourselves about ourselves and the world: all attitudes and responses which are only possible because of the fact that other humans have taught us to use reason and language. Secondly, we can conclude that socialisation is only possible because humans have specific abilities, biological "givens". These "givens" can vary from person to person and between the genders, but this does not make them less necessary conditions for the possibility of human society.

All the philosophers discussed in this book agree that male and female are by nature human beings and that our shared humanity is the basis on which relationships between the genders are built. I wish to point to this fact because I sometimes encounter statements to the effect that there are philosophers in the mainstream of the history of western philosophy who deny that women have rationality, souls, or humanity. This is a misunderstanding caused by reading philosophers on the wrong level. Philosophers often do claim that women are less rational and hence less "human" than men, but this distinction is not made on the fundamental plane of rationality, soul and humanity but on the secondary level of gender specific characteristics.

3   Gender Typing

I think that the most promising of present day attempts to answer questions concerning the patterns which occur in the creation of images of men and women, the nature-culture discussion, and the roles men and women are to have in society is the theory that people "gender type" themselves.[1] By "gender typing" is meant that people have a basic need to identify with a certain gender and this is done by describing and prescribing sexual roles, characteristics and ideals. The aim is to form sexual-social identity. Sexuality in this view is something which is not just given, but which is constantly expressed and reinforced in individual lives and in culture.

The main categories in which people place gender types are "male" and "female" for gender and "heterosexual" and "homosexual" for sexual orientation. Both categories are crude types because they may in fact be hopelessly inadequate for describing the wide variations which can occur in human gender identity and sexuality. What is interesting is that people want to *believe* that these categories apply and that they think that it is somehow important to classify human beings in this way. In gender typing, people create "ideal types" which are clear and easy to apply, aiding them in categorizing people and making their social-sexual world ordered and manageable. People attribute certain values and ideals to these types: a man who sees himself as fitting in the ideal category "male" feels he must live up to certain male images and he becomes convinced that he cannot then say that he would be just as well off with female ones. The perception of the value (a perception which can slide into a feeling of superiority) of one's own type is precisely the function of the exemplary nature of such images in the first place.

Gender typing can occur between men and women in order to identify a sexual mate as suitable and it can also occur in within groups of males or females themselves. People are evaluated within their own type on the basis of how "masculine" or "feminine" they seem to other members of the type. Gender typing can be used by a certain gender to make distinctions between people of that gender and certain typologies are presented to the other gender as attractive. The other gender in turn enforces, influences or changes the perception of what the ideal characteristics of the opposite sex are. Looking at this phenomenon from out of an evolutionary, sexual selection point of view, it means that men and women compete within their type and select outside of their type in such a way that certain characteristics of each gender are selected and passed on to the next generation.

Gender typing also plays a role in social-sexual development. Freud pointed out the importance of gender typing in the Oedipus and Electra phases of sexual development. Freud concentrated primarily on the pivotal nature of the first origins of sexual identification during what he calls the prehistorical phase in the life of a child, that is, the first three years of life.[2] At that age, the child's sexual orientation is developed through a complex reaction to its male and female role models, usually parents. In later variations on the Freudian theory of gender typing, created by his followers, the entire lifespan of people is seen as a process of sexual identification. In addition, Freud also pointed out that there are intellectual and cultural manifestations of gender typing which emerge through the process of sublimation. Culture can then be seen as both formed by sexual identification processes and in turn reinforcing the sexual identity of people.

If one wishes to account for differences in male-female nature and social roles in terms of the valuation of one's own type and the exclusion or downplaying of other types, the question remains as to what makes this process so incredibly powerful. Male-female cultural patterns and sex/gender taboos are so strong that they can be maintained over millennia. We often assume that if the creation and maintaining of such patterns is due to "nature" it means that the patterns are very set and difficult to change. But if we conclude that an important carrier of gender typing is culture, this means that culture, based on the expression of very fundamental human tendencies, is also extremely difficult to change. Perhaps culture, being so interdependent on nature is changed differently from the way nature changes but is equally difficult to change.

Feminism can be seen as an effort to alter gender typing rules and procedures. As we saw, Christine de Pizan, Mary Wollstonecraft and Luce Irigaray keep asking why women have been characterised in certain ways and excluded from certain realms. Feminists ask over and over again "why are women typed the way they are"? What enabled men to create certain ideologies about themselves and about women and why did women never manage to break through the exclusionary forces of the male system? As Simone de Beauvoir wonders, are there not two guilty parties, the men who created these images and the women who also created them and accepted them?[3]

Women have the distinct feeling that a number of characteristics which males appropriate to themselves (rationality or having careers, for example) are not specifically male characteristics at all and that male efforts to demonstrate that women are not good at these things or should not be participating in such activities at all are offensive. Feminists therefore wish to change the rules for typing male and female nature and social roles. But, assuming that despite the great strength of traditional typologies it is possible to change them, what criteria are there for such change? This is the issue with which society and feminism is now being faced.

4   Science and the Social Good

Who can and should how gender is to be typed and on what basis should such decisions be made? Men, women, science or the social-political agenda concerned with "the social good"? Women often claim that men have always been the ones who decided these matters and that this is not right or fair. Women themselves should have more of a voice in the gender typing process, a task many have taken on in western society. Is philosophy an area in which theories should be developed to support this effort or are we better off looking to other fields to arrive at answers? I will first look at two non-philosophical areas in which people look for answers to these questions and will then look at the efforts made in contemporary philosophy to analyse and promote the cause of women.

Are there scientifically "objective" criteria to settle the disputes? Perhaps scientific research could give neutral answers to what fits in best with male and female nature and what social-political role divisions would create a more perfect society? At the moment, a great amount of scientific research is being done in order to find factual answers to questions concerning male and female nature. Because of the complexity of the matter, science has not yet come to the point where it can give definitive answers.

It seems to me that the only general message coming out of scientific research is that a certain percentage of our make-up is different in male and female, a certain percentage the same. This is the case on both a genetic, biological level as well as on a social, intellectual level. Biologically, female and male are variations on one fundamental genetic pattern. Anthropological intercultural surveys have shown that males and females in widely varying cultures will show similar behavioural patterns and preferences but will differ in some respects due to cultural norms. Studies in cognitive theory and neurophysiology on the functioning of the brains of males and females show that males and females may make different use of some parts of their brains, accounting for phenomena such as the fact that males seem to be better in math, females in languages. On the other hand, not all males are better in math or worse in languages than all females and vice versa. It has also been shown that in different circumstances, for example, if males receive more attention with respect to language skills at school and females with math, the differences in test results also become smaller. These results would seem to confirm that there are no absolute differences between males and females and that influences on the functioning of the two genders is part nature, part culture.

Since research into areas such as biology, anthropology, cognitive theory and brain physiology apparently cannot at this time create firm theories to explain and predict the differences in the functioning of men and women, such research, when applied to everyday life, does not seem to be able to take us beyond the commonly held perception that describing gender differences takes us into a murky, grey area of sameness and difference. Perhaps what we need is a less scientific and more general and pragmatic means of distinguishing images and roles of men and women: we could look for criteria on a social-political level.

One could attempt to take one's point of departure in the concrete results of recent changes in gender roles in western culture and to project from that what the best way is to organise male and female roles in society in the future. But here too, we lack helpful answers. Our society is faced at present with a broad social agenda formulated by those who would like to give concrete expression to the notion of women's liberation. Some of the items on this agenda are: altering perceptions of social roles, having men care for children and the home, seeing to it that women are as well educated and as prepared for society as possible, helping women who get into difficulties with the male social and political order, and working on making society aware of damaging patterns of behaviour of males towards females. The problem with analysing this social agenda is that it does not form one coherent whole. Some of these initiatives serve to maintain traditional structures and serve the needs of women, for example, increased awareness of and protection against spousal abuse. Other points on the social agenda concern matters such as equal job opportunities, equal pay, and positive action to help women catch up with men in the workplace. It seems to me that pragmatism and responding to the needs of women governs the "progressive" social agenda, rather than abstract theories. This is of course a very good thing because it means that women are getting the practical support which they need. For theory formation, however, it becomes quite a muddle for someone looking for clear theories to determine what the leading ideas of such social reform are.

Another difficulty with using the present liberating social agenda to create guidelines for the future is that it is difficult to estimate what the impact is of the changes being made or their consequences for society and male-female relationships. Views on this differ widely. Some say that liberating women will mean the downfall of values, the family, and society. This seems to me an overly pessimistic view. Moreover, it is one-sided in the sense that it blames many social ills on the changing roles of mothers in the family while ignoring other factors which may lead to malaise in a society, including matters such as the economic situation of a country, job opportunities, declining values, and genera-tions of absent fathers. Others say the impact of women's liberation is not positive because in the end it will have only minimal results. Of those who say that, the most pessimistic view is that we need to do a great deal more to ensure that the process of the liberation of women is not bogged down or even turned back in ever changing social conditions and perceptions. Betty Friedan, for example, in her book *The Second Stage* warns against being overly optimistic about the achievements of the women's movement. She argues against optimism by referring to the historical lesson of the decline of the first feminist movement in the early years of our century, when women gained the right to vote. After that right was won, the women's movement declined, only being revived in the 1960's because of new social conditions in western countries.[4]

In the 1990's, Friedan's warning seems apt. There seems to be quite an onslaught on the women's movement at present. Outside the movement, a new image battle seems to have arisen, one which can be called in gender typing terminology "reverting to type". If gender typing depends on the creation of clear and stable types, as has been argued, there will be a strong tendency to reject complex variations on the type and to revert to old types. (This is the case not only in male-female typing but also in the related area mentioned at the beginning of this chapter, that of ethnicity). The result of this reversion is that feminists are once more being depicted as unattractive and out of date and/or that the people who were never convinced by feminism in the first place can now openly make this claim. In addition, the old strategy of "divide and conquer" has re-emerged. Women are being divided once more by the promise of equal opportunities and careers for those women who conform to increasingly conservative standards. Feminists have also been remorselessly attacked with the new catch phrase of the 90's, "political correctness". Under this label, feminism has been identified with petty tyranny arising from the desire to promote the interests of a minority; of reacting in an unreasonable way to the standards set up by a presumably reasonable, intelligent and tolerant society; and in its most extreme form, the political correctness attack takes the self-pitying form of a clearly powerful majority claiming to be themselves repressed by feminism. These tendencies are, moreover, not harmless rhetoric: the recent revoking of legislation concerning positive action in various states of the USA is a grim reminder to women and minorities that their social-political power is limited and hence that their rights can easily be taken away.

Besides the battle for ideas, images, and the future of society, women are (rightly or wrongly) internalising the social problems of our time and culture. The crumbling of social structures and of traditional morality in many western countries has led to neo-Conservative movements promising redemption in traditional family values and calling on women to uphold these values. Since women are once more being held responsible for the family and blamed for its failures, this places a burden on the feminist conscience. In addition, women themselves have have turned inward to reconsider their attitude towards family values for a practical reason: being faced with the toll on themselves of combining raising a family with a career.

These developments must surely serve as a warning that a lot still needs to be done to ensure that women have the freedom to determine their own lives and fate. We must once more be cautious about thinking that the battles for equal opportunities and equality have been won. At

the same time, the criticisms which have been made of feminism and
the practical difficulties resulting from some points on the feminist
agenda have served to moderate the movement. In our time, there is a
growing awareness on the part of feminism that there are no guarantees
that the course people set out to attain matters such as freedom and
equality will be the best course: women can only fight for what they
think is best. In the 1990's, the realisation has grown that there is no
gender utopia and no easy answers to be found by looking at the present
social situation.

5   The Task of Philosophy

In this climate, what can philosophy mean for the women's movement?
The discussion of the history of views of philosophers on women in this
book may help to analyse what some of the problems are in the way
men and women see each other and in the way they assign roles to each
other. In this sense, this book can be regarded as a consciousness raising
session. But what can philosophy mean for the women's movement in
the future? Can philosophy tell us whether the issues discussed in this
book will always be with us or if they can be resolved through social
change? Can it shed light on the question of whether women will remain
for a long time to come in the present limbo between traditional roles
and liberation from them?

   Philosophy can contribute to the women's movement by analysing
theoretically what is going on in society and in those areas in which
academic research on women is being done. Besides taking up the role
of diagnostician, the philosopher can also attempt to develop theories
on women within all the various philosophical fields. Perhaps the most
worthwhile and challenging task for philosophers is the creation of a
philosophical ethics of how to see women and their roles in society.
Philosophers on the whole have felt so threatened by the women's
movement that they have failed to understand that the primary impulse
of this movement is an ethical one. In this sense, the women's movement
is part of the more general social tendency to realise ethical ideals by
fighting for specific causes. Examples of this tendency is the support
people give to Amnesty International, the environmental movement,
and the development of the third world.[5]

Can philosophy aid both society and the women's movement by developing an "ethics of sexual difference", to quote Irigaray? Philosophy cannot and may not tell people what to do, but because of its theoretical strength, it can aid in clarifying ethical positions and formulating which values would fit into a consistent pattern and argue for the importance of having certain values. In the present philosophical debate, two positions are already crystalizing. One is the choice for traditional liberal values such as freedom of speech, respect for others, and the freedom of self-expression and self-fulfillment, free from domination. Another option is to argue for an ethics of compassion, concern and care, an ethics of self-sacrifice, which can form the basis for male-female relationships as well as the attitude of people to others in society.

There are, however, a number of drawbacks to such a project. In the first place, philosophy has, as Hegel pointed out, the woeful fate of always coming into action after the event. Whether philosophical-theoretical purists like it or not, society and interest groups inside it are already diagnosing problems and making decisions to solve them. This is of course a good thing because society cannot wait for philosophy to come up with solutions. Besides, the fact that philosophy comes after the event can be an advantage because it can then place practise in the context of theory. A second difficulty is that the male philosophical establishment is not very interested in supporting the development of an ethics of sexual difference because it is seen as something women should develop in their own philosophical sub-class and which only applies to them. Men have the tendency to apply themselves to these matters only when they feel that there is either status at stake or a crisis which needs their attention. In all other cases, women are seen as responsible for theory formation on women, the family, and the role of women in society. Lastly, another barrier to overcome is to create a philosophy which applies to all women, not only a small number of well-educated middle class western women. Is it possible to create a philosophical ethics of sexual difference which would transcend these boundaries?

The task of philosophy in theoretically supporting and furthering the women's movement is, luckily, not something which has to begin from point zero. It has been argued that the most revolutionary, pervasive movement for change in western society in the latter part of the 20th century has been the women's movement. This movement can provide philosophers with a vast resource of new theoretical concepts. The task of philosophy is to take up these concepts and to make something of them which will provide society with a solid theoretical basis for its decisions on male and female.

Women today owe much to the women's movement, whether they regard themselves as part of that movement or not. The women's movement has been a great ethical accomplishment because it has succeeded in identifying and to some extent taking down the barriers that have been put up for women in the public realm. It is also responsible for the creation of more positive self-images of women. Men have learned to accept women as more equal to them than in the past and hopefully will continue to make progress in this area. Women can rightly be proud of having brought about these changes, for many of them have been due to their own efforts, hard fought for by women for themselves and for other women.

Notes

1 J.G.M. de Bruijn, "Controversial Quality", in: J.G.M. de Bruijn, L.D. Derksen, C.M.J. Hoeberichts, ed., *The Women's Movement: History and Theory*. Aldershot, England, Avebury Press, 1993, p. 61-82.

2 L. Irigaray, *Speculum. Of the Other Woman*. transl. by Gillian C. Gill. Ithaca, New York, Cornell University Press, 1985, p. 41-43, p. 64.

3 S. de Beauvoir, "Introduction" to: *The Second Sex*. New York, Bantam Books, 1954/1970.

4 Betty Friedan, *The Second Stage*. London, Michael Joseph, 1981.

5 D.C. Dennett, in an interview in W. Kaiser's film series *Een schitterend ongeluk*, 1992, notes that traditional philosophical ethics has undergone changes in the last decades. Ethics has become not the formulating of abstract, general principles, but fighting for specific causes.

Bibliography

Amsberg, K. Interview with L. Irigaray, "Al eeuwen lang leven wij in de verhouding moeder-zoon", in: *Denken over liefde en macht*. Amsterdam, van Gennep, 1982. p. 113-127.

Aquinas, St. Thomas. *The Summa Theologica.* transl. by the Fathers of the English Dominican Province. London, Burns, Oates and Washbourne, 1911.

"Ariadne", *Ariadne Jahrbuch der Nietzsche Gesellschaft* 1925, p. 5-6.

Aristotle. *The Works of Aristotle.* transl. and ed. by W.D. Ross. Oxford, Clarendon Press, 1952.

Assaad-Mikhail, F. "Kierkegaard interprète de Nietzsche". *Revue de Métaphysique et de Morale* 78 (1973, Ja/Mr), p. 45-87.

St. Augustine, *Confessions.* transl. by V.J. Bourke. The Fathers of the Church. Washington, Catholic University of America Press, 1953. Vol. 21.

Bacon, Francis, *Works.* Collected and edited by J. Spedding, R.L. Ellis and D.D. Heath. Stuttgart, Fromann, 1961-1963. 14 vol.

de Beauvoir, S. *The Second Sex.* New York, Bantam Books, 1970 [1952].

Beerling, R.F. *Het cultuurprotest van Jean-Jacques Rousseau. Studies over het thema pathos en nostalgie.* Deventer, van Lochum Slaterus, 1977.

Blok, H.P. *Opmerkingen over het gevoel van het schone en verhevene.* Sneek, van Druten, 1919. Annotated Dutch translation of I. Kant, *Beobachtungen über das Gefühl des Schönen und Erhabenen.*

Brody, Miriam. "Mary Wollstonecraft: Sexuality and Women's Rights (1759-1797)". in: Dale Spender, ed. *Feminist Theorists. Three Centuries of Key Women Thinkers.* New York/Toronto, Random House, 1983. p. 40-59.

de Bruijn, J., Derksen, L.D., Hoeberichts, I. eds. *The Women's Movement, History and Theory.* Hampstead, England, Avebury Press, 1993.

Capelle, Catherine. *Thomas D'Aquin Féministe?* Paris, Vrin, 1982.

Christine de Pizan. *The Book of the City of Ladies.* transl. by E.J. Richards. Foreword by M. Warner. New York, Persea Books, 1982. First published between 1405-1407.

Clark, L. and Lange, L., eds. *The Sexism of Social and Political Theory: Women and Reproduction from Plato to Nietzsche.* Toronto, University of Toronto Press, 1979.

de Costa, Denise, *Sprekende Stiltes.* Kampen, Kok, 1989.

Curnow, M. *The "Livre de la cité des dames" of Christine de Pisan.* Ann Arbor Michigan, USA, University Microfilms International; London, England, 1975. 2 volumes.

Dalitz, R.J. "Towards a Feminist Analysis of Patriarchal Logic", in: M. Pellikaan-Engel, ed., *Against Patriarchal Thinking.* Amsterdam, VU University Press, 1992, p. 35-40.

Derksen, L.D. "De feministische filosofie van Luce Irigaray", *Beweging* 48 (1984, 6), p. 107-109.

Derksen, L.D. "Catherine Capelle: Thomas d'Aquin Féministe?", *Stoichea* I (1986, 3), p. 63-68.

Derksen, L.D. "The Ambiguous Relationship Between Feminism and Postmo-dernism", in: M. Pellikaan-Engel, ed., *Against Patriarchal Thinking.* Amsterdam, VU University Press, 1992, p. 131-140.

Derksen, L.D. "Luce Irigaray. Het denken van differentie". H.E.S. Woldring, ed., *Moderne franse filosofen.* Kampen, Kok, 1993. p. 46-63.

Deleuze, Gilles. "Mystère d'Ariane". *Bulletin de la Societé Française d'Études Nietzschéennes* 2 (1973, March), p. 12-15.

Derrida, Jacques. *Spurs/Éperons. Nietzsche's Styles/Les Styles de Nietzsche.* transl. by B. Harlow. Chicago/London, University of Chicago Press, 1978.

Derrida, Jacques. *On Grammatology.* transl. with and introduction by G.C. Spivak. Baltimore/London, Johns Hopkins University Press, 1974, 1976.

Descartes, René. *The Philosophical Works of Descartes.* transl. by Elisabeth S. Haldane and G.T.R. Ross. Cambridge, Cambridge University Press, 1973, 1976. 2 volumes.

Descartes, René. *Descartes. His Moral Philosophy and Psychology.* transl. with an intro. by John J. Blom. Hassocks, Sussex, Harvester Press, 1978.

Echeverria, E. *Criticism and Commitment. Major Themes in Contemporary `Post-Critical' Philosophy.* Amsterdam, Rodopi, 1981.

Elshtain, J.B. *Public Man, Private Woman: Women in Social and Political Thought.* Princeton, Princeton University Press, 1981.

Farrington, B. *Francis Bacon: Philosopher of Industrial Science.* New York, Schumann, 1949.

Flax, Jane. "Political Philosophy and the Patriarchal Unconscious: A Psychoanalytic Perspective on Epistemology and Metaphysics", in: S. Harding and M. Hintikka, *Discovering Reality.* Dordrecht, Reidel, 1983. p. 245-281.

Fortenbaugh, W.W. "Aristotle on Slaves and Women", in: J. Barnes et. al., eds, *Articles on Aristotle. Vol. 2: Ethics and Politics.* London, Duckworth, 1977. p. 135-139.

Freud, S. *The Standard Edition of the Complete Psychological Works of Sigmund Freud.* ed. by J. Strachey. London, Hogarth Press, 1953-1974, 24 vols.

Friedan, B. *The Second Stage.* London, Michael Joseph, 1981.

Goreau, Angeline. "Alphra Behn: A Scandal to Modesty", in: D. Spender, ed. *Feminist Theorists. Three Centuries of Key Women Thinkers.* New York/Toronto, Random House, 1983, p. 8-27.

Garside, Christine. "Can a Woman be Good in the Same Way as a Man?", *Dialogue* 10 (1971), p. 534-544.

Gatens, Moira. "Rousseau and Wollstonecraft: Nature versus Reason", *Australasian Journal of Philosophy,* Supplement to vol. 64, June 1986. p. 1-15.

Van der Haegen, Rina. *In het spoor van de seksuele differentie.* Nijmegen, SUN, 1989.

Harding, S., and Hintikka, M., eds., *Discovering Reality: Feminist Perspectives on Epistemology, Metaphysics, Methodology and the Philosophy of Science.* Dordrecht, Reidel, 1983.

Harding, Sandra. "Is Gender a Variable in Conceptions of Rationality? A Survey of Issues". *Dialectica* 36 (1982, 2/3), p. 225-242.

Hegel, G.F.W. *Phenomenology of Spirit.* transl. by A.V. Miller. Oxford, Oxford University Press, 1977.

Hegel, G.F.W. *Hegel's Philosophy of Right.* transl. and annotated by T.M. Knox. London/Oxford, Oxford University Press, 1967.

Heijst, A. van. *Verlangen naar de val.* Kampen, Kok, 1992.

Hildegard von Bingen. *Welt und Mensch.* ed. by Heinrich Schipperges. Salzburg, Otto Müller Verlag, 1965.

Hildegard von Bingen. *Wisse die Wege. (Scivias).* ed. by Maura Böckeler. Salzburg, Otto Müller Verlag, 1954.

Hochschild, Arlie. *The Second Shift.* Viking, 1989.

Hollingdale, R.J. "Introduction" to F. Nietzsche, *Thus Spoke Zarathustra.* London, Penguin, 1961/1969, p. 11-35.

Horowitz, Maryanne Cline. "Aristotle on Woman". *Journal of the History of Biology* 9 (1976,2), p. 183-213.

Hume, David. *Essays. Philosophical Works.* ed. by Green and Grose, vol. 4. (first published in 1742 and 1748, Edinburgh)

Hume, David. *A Treatise of Human Nature.* ed. by L.A. Selby-Bigge. Oxford, Oxford University Press, 1978- 2. (first published in 1739-1740).

Irigaray, Luce. *Le langage des déments.* The Hague/Paris, Éditions Mouton, 1973.

Irigaray, Luce. *Speculum. De l'autre femme.* Paris, Minuit, 1974. English translation: *Speculum. Of the Other Woman.* transl. by Gilian C. Gill. Ithaca, New York, Cornell University Press, 1985.

Irigaray, Luce. *Ce sexe qui n'en est pas un.* Paris, Éditions de Minuit, 1977. English translation: *This Sex Which Is Not One.* transl. by Catherine Porter with Carolyn Burke. Ithaca, New York, Cornell University Press, 1985.

Irigaray, Luce. *Et l'une ne bouge pas sans l'autre.* Paris, Minuit, 1979.

Irigaray, Luce. *Amante Marine. De Friedrich Nietzsche.* Paris, Minuit, 1980.

Irigaray, Luce. *Le corps-à-corps avec la mère.* Montréal, Les éditions de la pleine lune, 1981.

Irigaray, Luce. Interview with Luce Irigaray, "Al eeuwen leven wij in de verhouding moeder-zoon". *Denken over liefde en macht.* Amsterdam, van Gennep, 1982. p. 113-127. (Dutch)

Irigaray, Luce. Interview with Luce Irigaray in *NRC Handelsblad,* Nov. 25, 1982: "Vrouwen weten dat de waarheid niet bestaat".

Irigaray, Luce. *Passions élémentaires.* Paris, Minuit, 1982.

Irigaray, Luce. *La Croyance Même.* Paris, Galileé, 1983.

Irigaray, Luce. *Éthique de la différence sexuelle* (dual French/Dutch edition, however not same as book of same title noted under Irigaray 1984). transl. by J. Buntinx, A. Vincenot, R. Weber. Rotterdam, Centrale Interfaculteit Erasmus University, 1983.

Irigaray, Luce. *L'Oubli de l'air.* Paris, Minuit, 1983.

Irigaray, Luce. *Éthique de la différence sexuelle.* Paris, Minuit, 1984.

Irigaray, Luce. *Parler n'est jamais neutre*. Paris, Minuit, 1985.

Irigaray, Luce. *Le temps de la différence*. Paris, Grasset, 1989.

Irigaray, Luce. *Je, tu, nous: pour une culture de la différence*. Paris, Editions Grasset et Fasquelle, 1990. English translation: *Je, tu, nous: Toward a Culture of Difference*. New York, Routledge, 1993.

Kant, Immanuel. *Beobachtungen über das Gefühl des Schönen und Erhabenen*, in: W. Weischedel, ed. *I. Kant. Werke*. Darmstadt, Wissenschaftliche Buchgesellschaft, 1960. Volume I, *Vorkritische Schriften bis 1768*, p. 825-884. English translation: *Observations on the Feeling of the Beautiful and the Sublime*. transl. by John T. Goldthwait. Berkeley, Los Angeles, University of California Press, 1960. (first published in 1764, Königsberg).

Lange, Lynda. "Rousseau: Women and the General Will", in: L. Clarke and L. Lange, eds., *The Sexism of Social and Political Theory: Women and Reproduction from Plato to Nietzsche*. Toronto, University of Toronto Press, 1979. p. 41-52.

Lange, Lynda. "Woman is not a Rational Animal: On Aristotle's Biology of Reproduction", in: S. Harding and M. Hintikka, *Discovering Reality*. Dordrecht, Reidel, 1983. p. 1-15.

Lloyd, Genevieve. "Masters, Slaves and Others", *Radical Philosophy* 34 (1983, Summer), p. 1-9.

Lloyd, Genevieve. *The Man of Reason. "Male" and "Female" in Western Philosophy*. London, Methuen, 1984.

Lukács, Georg. *Die Zerstörung der Vernunft*. Berlin, Aufbau-Verlag, 1954.

Malet, Nicole. "L'homme et la femme dans la philosophie de Nietzsche", *Revue de Métaphysique et de Morale* 82 (1977, Ja./Mr.), p. 38-63.

Matthews, Gareth B. "Gender and Essence in Aristotle", *Australasian Journal of Philosophy*, Supplement to vol. 64, June 1986. p. 16-25.

McLaughlin, Eleanor Commo, "Equality of Souls, Inequality of Sexes: Woman in Medieval Theology", in: Rosemary Radford Reuther, ed., *Religion and Sexism*. New York, Simon and Schuster, 1974, p. 213-266.

Ménage, Gilles. *The History of Women Philosophers*. transl. with an intro. by Beatrice H. Zedler. Lanham/London, University Press of America, 1984. (original title, *Historia Mulierum Philosopharum*, 1690/1692).

Merchant, Carolyn. *The Death of Nature*. New York, Harper and Row, 1980.

Nicholson, Linda, ed. *Feminism/Postmodernism*. New York/London, Routledge, 1990.

Nietzsche, F. *Nietzsches Werke*. ed. by Gerhard Stenzel. Salzburg, Bergland, 2 volumes.

Nietzsche, F. *Thus Spoke Zarathustra*. transl. by R.J. Hollingdale. London, Penguin, 1961/1969.

Ormiston, Gayle L. "Traces of Derrida: Nietzsche's Image of Woman", *Philosophy Today* (1984, Summer), p. 178-188.

Patton, Paul, ed., *Nietzsche, Feminism and Political Theory*. London, Routledge, 1993.

Pellikaan-Engel, Maja. "Socrates' Blind Spots", in: M. Pellikaan-Engel, ed., *Against Patriarchal Thinking*. Amsterdam, VU University Press, 1992, p. 5-11. This is a revised and shortened version of the original article, "De verhouding Socrates-Xanthippe in filosofisch perspectief", *Feminisme Filosofie*. Leusden, Internationale school voor wijsbegeerte, 1979. p. 7-28.

Pellikaan-Engel, Maja, ed., *Against Patriarchal Thinking*. Amsterdam, VU University Press, 1992.

Peters, H. F. *My Sister, My Spouse*. New York, W.W. Norton, 1962.

Philo of Alexandria. *Complete Works*. transl. by H. Colson and H. Whitaker. Loeb Classical Library, 1952.

Plato, *Collected Dialogues*. transl. by Hamilton and Cairns. Princeton, Princeton University Press, 1973.

Ponfoort, Tine. "Introduction" to the Dutch translation of Christine de Pizan, *Le livre de la Cité des Dames: Het Boek van de Stad der Vrouwen*. Amsterdam, Nijgh & Van Ditmar, 1984, p. 7-17.

Quinot, Armand. "Notes: Ariane". *Bulletin de la Société Française d'Études Nietzschéennes* 2 (1963, March), p. 16-18.

Radford Ruether, Rosemary. "Misogynism and Virginal Feminism in the Fathers of the Church", in: Rosemary Radford Ruether, ed., *Religion and Sexism*. New York, Simon and Schuster, 1974, p. 150-183.

Riessen, Renée van, *Antigone's bruidsvertrek. De plaats van de Antigone in Hegels denken over de vrouw*. Kampen, Kok, 1986.

Rich, Adrienne, *Of Woman Born*. New York, W.W. Norton, 1976.

Rousseau, Jean-Jacques, *Emile.* transl. by Allan Bloom. New York, Basic Books, 1979. (first published in 1762).

Rousseau, Jean-Jacques, *Confessions.* Baltimore, Penguin Books, 1967.

Salomé, Lou Andreas. *Friedrich Nietzsche in seinen Werken.* Dresden, Carl Reissner. (Reprint of the first edition of 1894.)

Schopenhauer, Arthur. *Essays and Aphorisms.* Selected and Translated with an Introduction by R.J. Hollingdale. Harmondsworth, Middlesex, England, Penguin, 1970/1985. Selections from *Parerga and Paralipomena.* (First published in 1851.)

Spelman, Elisabeth. "Aristotle and the Politicization of the Soul", S. Harding and M. Hintikka, eds. *Discovering Reality.* Dordrecht, Reidel, 1983. p. 17-30.

Spender, Dale, ed. *Feminist Theorists. Three Centuries of Key Women Thinkers.* New York/Toronto, Random House, 1983.

Thesleff, Holger. *An Introduction to the Pythagorean Writings of the Hellenistic Period.* Acta Academiae Aboensis xxiv.3. Abo, 1961.

Thompson, Janna. "Women and the High Priests of Reason", *Radical Philosophy* 34 (1983, Summer), p. 10-14.

Waithe, Mary Ellen, ed. *A History of Women Philosophers.* Vol.1: 600 B.C.-500 A.D. Dordrecht/ London/ Lancaster, Martinus Nijhoff, 1987.

Wardle, R.M. "Introduction" to *The Collected Letters of Mary Wollstonecraft.* Ithaca/London, Cornell University Press, 1979. p. 27-50.

Warren, M.A. ed. *The Nature of Woman.* Inverness, California, Edgepress, 1980.

Wender, D. "Plato: Mysoginist, Paedophile, and Feminist", *Arethusa* 6 (1973), p. 75-90.

Willard, C.C. *Christine de Pizan. Her Life and Works.* New York, Persea Books, 1984.

Williams, Bernard. "Descartes, René", in: P. Edwards, ed. *The Encyclopedia of Philosophy.* New York/London, MacMillan and the Free Press/Collier MacMillan, 1967. Volume 2, p. 344-354.

Wollstonecraft, Mary. *Collected Letters of Mary Wollstonecraft.* Ithaca/London, Cornell University Press, 1979.

Wollstonecraft, Mary. *A Vindication of the Rights of Woman.* London, Dent, 1929/1977. (first published in 1792).